DORDOGNE

TRAVEL GUIDE

2024

Discover Historic Landmarks, Must-See
Attractions, Cuisine, Activities, Accommodation
Options, Insider Tips and Itinerary for an
Unforgettable Adventure in Southern France

Jeff Sowell

D1739089

TABLE OF CONTENTS

INTRODUCTION

In the beautiful region of Dordogne, France, lies a world waiting to be discovered. It's a place where ancient history meets modern adventure, where every corner holds a new surprise. I am excited to share my journey of exploration through Dordogne with you and provide a comprehensive and engaging companion for your own adventure to this magical destination.

My fascination with Dordogne began long before I stepped foot on its storied terrain. I had heard tales of its medieval castles, charming villages, and lush vineyards, and these stories sparked an insatiable wanderlust within me. From the moment I arrived, I was swept away by the timeless charm of Sarlat-la-Canéda, a town where history comes alive. Stone houses basked in the sun, surrounded by colorful flower boxes and narrow alleyways. Wandering through its maze-like streets, I found myself transported back in time, imagining the knights and nobles who once roamed these same cobblestones. Every twist and turn revealed a new architectural marvel, from Gothic cathedrals to half-timbered houses adorned with colorful shutters.

Yet, it was not just the landmarks that captured my heart; it was the people of Dordogne who truly made my experience unforgettable. From the jovial market vendors who greeted me with smiles and samples of their wares to the passionate artisans who shared their craft with me, I was welcomed into the fabric of daily life in Dordogne with open arms. Whether I was sipping wine with a local winemaker or learning the art of truffle hunting from a seasoned expert, I was constantly reminded of the warmth and generosity that define the spirit of this region.

Of course, no visit to Dordogne would be complete without indulging in its world-renowned cuisine. From rustic country fare to haute cuisine, every meal was a feast for the senses, a celebration of the region's rich gastronomic heritage. I delighted in the earthy flavors of truffles, the velvety richness of foie gras, and the savory goodness of duck confit, each dish a testament to the culinary mastery that has been passed down through generations.

The hills and rivers of Dordogne aren't just scenery; they're invitations to explore. Kayaking down the Dordogne River, I discovered hidden coves and lush forests, each bend revealing a new breathtaking view. But Dordogne isn't just about landscapes and food; it's a living museum of history. Exploring the Lascaux IV caves, I was amazed by the ancient artwork that connected me to our earliest ancestors.

Dordogne isn't simply a destination stumbled upon online; rather, it's a place that reveals itself to you. As I sit here reflecting, I'm enveloped by the warmth of the sun and the soft rustle of the breeze weaving through the trees. It's in moments like these that I realize the internet fails to capture the true essence of this remarkable region. Dordogne is a treasure trove of history, breathtaking scenery, and genuine warmth that must be experienced firsthand to be fully appreciated.

Let this guide be your trusted companion as you navigate the charming towns and hidden corners of Dordogne. From planning your trip and choosing the perfect accommodations to uncovering the region's cultural treasures, I've curated every section with care, ensuring that you have the most fulfilling and unforgettable experience possible.

Whether you're an intrepid adventurer seeking the thrill of exploring historic sites, a family looking for a fun-filled vacation, a couple seeking a romantic escape, or a nature enthusiast eager to immerse yourself in the region's natural beauty, Dordogne has something extraordinary to offer every traveler. Let your senses be captivated by the charm of this enchanting region, and allow yourself to be enchanted by its timeless allure.

As you turn the pages of this guide, I hope you feel the same sense of wonder and excitement that I felt during my own journey. May it inspire you to create your own cherished memories, forge new connections with the world around you, and uncover the hidden gems that make Dordogne a truly unrivaled destination.

So, without further delay, let's embark on this adventure together. From the pages of this travel guide to the stunning landscapes that await you, may your trip to Dordogne be nothing short of extraordinary. Prepare to be captivated, inspired, and forever changed by this remarkable region. I promise, you won't want to leave.

About Dordogne

Dordogne, settled in the southwestern part of France, is a region steeped in natural beauty, rich history, and culinary delights. Known for its picturesque landscapes, charming villages, and prehistoric sites, Dordogne offers a unique blend of adventure and tranquility for visitors.

The region boasts rolling hills, lush forests, and meandering rivers, providing a stunning backdrop for outdoor activities such as hiking, cycling, and canoeing. The Dordogne River, in particular, is a popular destination for kayaking and boating, offering breathtaking views of towering cliffs and hidden caves along its banks.

Dordogne is also renowned for its prehistoric sites, including the famous Lascaux caves with their remarkable cave paintings dating back thousands of years. Visitors can explore these ancient wonders and gain insight into the lives of early humans who once inhabited the region.

In addition to its natural and historical attractions, Dordogne is a paradise for food lovers. The region is known for its gastronomic delights, including foie gras, truffles, and duck confit. Visitors can indulge in traditional French cuisine at local restaurants and markets, sampling dishes made with fresh, locally sourced ingredients.

But Dordogne is not just about outdoor adventures and culinary delights; it also offers a glimpse into French village life. Quaint villages like Sarlat-la-Canéda and Rocamadour are adorned with charming stone houses, cobblestone streets, and bustling markets, providing a taste of authentic French culture and hospitality.

Whether you're seeking outdoor adventures, cultural experiences, or simply a relaxing getaway, Dordogne has something to offer everyone. With its timeless beauty and rich heritage, it's no wonder that Dordogne continues to captivate visitors from around the world.

Why you should Visit Dordogne

There are countless reasons why Dordogne should be on your travel radar. Here are some compelling reasons why you should consider visiting this captivating region:

1. Stunning Scenery: Dordogne boasts breathtaking natural landscapes, including rolling hills, meandering rivers, and lush forests. Whether you're hiking through the countryside or simply soaking in the views, the beauty of Dordogne will leave you spellbound.

2. Rich History: Dordogne is steeped in history, with prehistoric sites dating back thousands of years. From the famous Lascaux caves with their ancient cave paintings to the medieval castles and fortified villages that dot the landscape, the region offers a fascinating glimpse into the past.

3. Charming Villages: Explore charming villages with their quaint cobblestone streets, historic architecture, and lively markets. Places like Sarlat-la-Canéda and Rocamadour exude old-world charm and offer a chance to experience traditional French village life.

4. Culinary Delights: Indulge your taste buds in the gastronomic delights of Dordogne. The region is known for its delicious cuisine, including foie gras, truffles, duck confit, and walnut cake. Sample local delicacies at bustling markets, cozy bistros, and Michelin-starred restaurants.

5. Outdoor Adventures: Dordogne is a paradise for outdoor enthusiasts. From hiking and cycling to kayaking and canoeing, there are endless opportunities to explore the great outdoors. Discover hidden trails, scenic rivers, and panoramic viewpoints as you embark on your adventure.

6. Cultural Experiences: Immerse yourself in the vibrant culture of Dordogne. Attend festivals, concerts, and art exhibitions that showcase the region's rich artistic heritage. Visit museums, galleries, and cultural sites to learn about the history and traditions of Dordogne.

7. Warm Hospitality: Experience the warm hospitality of the people of Dordogne. Whether you're interacting with locals at a market or being welcomed into a family-run bed and breakfast, you'll find that the people of Dordogne are friendly, welcoming, and eager to share their love for their region.

In summary, Dordogne offers a unique blend of natural beauty, rich history, culinary delights, and outdoor adventures that make it a must-visit destination. Whether you're seeking relaxation, adventure, or cultural experiences, Dordogne has something for everyone. So why wait? Start planning your trip to Dordogne today and discover the magic of this enchanting region for yourself.

History and Cultural Overview

Dordogne, situated in the southwest of France, boasts a rich and varied history that spans thousands of years. From prehistoric cave paintings to medieval castles and Renaissance architecture, the region is a treasure trove of cultural heritage.

Prehistoric Origins:
Dordogne is renowned for its prehistoric sites, most notably the Lascaux caves. Discovered in 1940, these caves contain some of the finest examples of Paleolithic cave art in the world, dating back over 17,000 years. The intricate paintings

depict animals such as horses, deer, and bulls, providing a fascinating glimpse into the lives of our ancient ancestors.

Medieval Times:
During the Middle Ages, Dordogne was a region of strategic importance, dotted with fortified castles and bastide towns. Many of these medieval fortifications still stand today, serving as reminders of the region's tumultuous past. The town of Sarlat-la-Canéda, with its beautifully preserved medieval architecture, is a prime example of Dordogne's medieval heritage.

Renaissance and Enlightenment:
In the 16th and 17th centuries, Dordogne experienced a period of cultural and artistic flourishing. Renaissance châteaux, such as the Château de Beynac and the Château de Castelnaud, were built along the Dordogne River, showcasing the wealth and power of the region's noble families. The Enlightenment also left its mark on Dordogne, with the establishment of academies and cultural institutions that promote intellectual and artistic pursuits.

Modern Era:
In more recent history, Dordogne has evolved into a vibrant cultural hub, attracting artists, writers, and musicians from around the world. The region's picturesque landscapes and charming villages continue to inspire creativity, while its rich culinary heritage delights food enthusiasts from far and wide.

Cultural Traditions:
Dordogne is also known for its rich cultural traditions, including music, dance, and folklore. Traditional festivals such

as the Félibrée celebrate the region's Occitan heritage, with lively parades, music, and dance performances.

Overall, Dordogne's history and cultural heritage are as diverse and fascinating as its landscapes. Whether you're exploring ancient cave paintings, wandering through medieval castles, or sampling the region's culinary delights, Dordogne offers a rich tapestry of experiences that will captivate and inspire visitors of all ages.

CHAPTER 1.

PLANNING YOUR TRIP

Planning your trip to Dordogne is the key to a smooth and enjoyable experience. This chapter covers everything you need to know to prepare for your adventure. From choosing the best time to visit and booking your accommodation to understanding transportation options and packing essentials, careful planning will ensure you make the most of your time in this beautiful region. Get ready to explore Dordogne's rich history, stunning landscapes, and delicious cuisine with confidence and ease.

When to visit Dordogne

Dordogne, with its enchanting landscapes and rich cultural heritage, is a destination that beckons travelers year-round. Each season brings its own unique charm, offering visitors a different perspective on this picturesque region of France. Here's a guide to help you choose the perfect time to visit Dordogne:

Spring (March to May):
As the winter chill fades away, Dordogne bursts into life with the arrival of spring. The countryside awakens with vibrant colors as wildflowers bloom and trees blossom. Now is the ideal moment to investigate the region's charming villages and medieval castles, with the weather mild and pleasant for outdoor activities like hiking and cycling. This is the perfect time to visit local markets and sample fresh produce, as spring brings an abundance of seasonal delights to Dordogne's culinary scene.

Summer (June to August):

Summer is the peak tourist season in Dordogne, and for good reason. The long, sunny days provide the ideal setting for outdoor pursuits, from kayaking along the Dordogne River to picnicking in the shade of ancient oak trees. The region comes alive with festivals, concerts, and outdoor markets, offering visitors a taste of Dordogne's vibrant cultural scene. While temperatures can be warm during the day, the evenings are pleasantly cool, making alfresco dining a delightful experience.

Autumn (September to November):

As summer fades into autumn, Dordogne is transformed by a riot of colors when the foliage changes hue. The countryside is bathed in golden light, creating a picturesque backdrop for leisurely walks and scenic drives. Autumn is also harvest season in Dordogne, with vineyards and orchards bursting with ripe fruits and grapes. Guests can take part in grape harvests, wine tastings, and truffle hunts, immersing themselves in the region's rich culinary traditions.

Winter (December to February):

Wintertime arrives with a quiet, magical charm to Dordogne, with fewer tourists and a peaceful atmosphere. The countryside takes on a serene beauty, with frost-covered fields and mist-shrouded valleys creating a scene straight out of a fairy tale. While outdoor activities may be limited due to the cooler temperatures, winter is the perfect time to cozy up by the fireplace in a traditional gîte or farmhouse, savoring hearty meals and local wines. Don't miss the chance to explore

Dordogne's historic sites and museums, which take on a special allure in the quieter winter months.

Ultimately, The ideal time to visit Dordogne may depend on your interests. and interests. Whether you're looking for peaceful activities, cultural encounters, or outdoor adventures getaway, Dordogne possesses something to give year-round. So gather your belongings and set out to explore the timeless beauty and rich heritage of this captivating region.

Entry and visa requirements

Before embarking on your dream adventure to dordogne, it's essential to understand the entry and visa requirements for visiting this enchanting region. Dordogne, located in the heart of France, welcomes visitors from around the globe with open arms, but a few formalities must be addressed beforehand.

When it comes to entering Dordogne, travelers from many countries, including members of the European Union, the United States, Canada, Australia, and Japan, can enjoy visa-free travel for short stays of up to 90 days within a 180-day period. This lenient policy allows for ample time to explore the region's myriad attractions without the hassle of obtaining a visa in advance.

However, it's crucial to ensure that your passport remains valid for at least six months beyond your planned date of departure from Dordogne. Additionally, travelers should possess proof of onward travel arrangements, such as a return ticket or itinerary, to demonstrate their intention to depart the country within the allotted time frame.

For citizens of countries not covered by visa-free travel agreements, obtaining a Schengen visa is a prerequisite for visiting Dordogne. The Schengen visa, valid for stays of up to 90 days within a 180-day period, grants entry not only to France but also to 25 other European countries within the Schengen Area. To obtain a Schengen visa, applicants must submit a comprehensive set of documents, including a completed application form, a valid passport, travel itinerary, proof of accommodation, travel insurance, and evidence of sufficient financial means to support their stay.

Once these requirements are met, travelers can embark on their Dordogne adventure, ready to immerse themselves in the region's rich cultural heritage, breathtaking landscapes, and delectable cuisine. Whether wandering the cobblestone streets of medieval villages, sampling local delicacies at bustling markets, or exploring ancient chateaux settled amidst rolling vineyards, Dordogne promises an unforgettable experience for every visitor.

Before setting off on your journey to Dordogne, ensure that you comply with the entry and visa requirements applicable to your country of origin. With proper preparation and documentation in hand, you'll be well-equipped to savor all that this enchanting region has to offer, creating memories to last a lifetime.

Accommodation Options in Dordogne

Dordogne, with its rich history, picturesque landscapes, and vibrant culture, offers a diverse range of accommodation options to suit every traveler's preferences and budget. From luxurious châteaux to charming bed and breakfasts, here's a comprehensive guide to help you find the perfect place to stay during your visit to this enchanting region:

1. Châteaux:

Dordogne is renowned for its stunning châteaux, which offer a glimpse into the region's rich architectural heritage and aristocratic past. Many of these magnificent properties have been transformed into elegant hotels, offering guests a unique blend of history, luxury, and charm. Here are three notable châteaux in Dordogne:

a. Château de la Treyne
Address: Lacave, 46200, France

Château de la Treyne is a magnificent hotel set in a historic castle overlooking the Dordogne River. The castle features elegant rooms with period decor, a gourmet restaurant serving exquisite French cuisine, and beautifully landscaped gardens. Guests can enjoy stunning river views, take leisurely walks in the expansive grounds, and indulge in luxurious amenities, including an outdoor pool and tennis courts. The serene atmosphere and exceptional service make it a perfect destination for a romantic getaway or a relaxing retreat.

Directions: To get there, take the D820 road from Souillac towards Martel, then follow signs for Lacave.

b. Château des Milandes (Address: 24250 Castelnaud-la-Chapelle, France):

Once the home of Josephine Baker, Château des Milandes is a beautifully restored Renaissance castle set amidst vineyards and woodlands. Visitors can explore the castle's opulent interiors, stroll through the manicured gardens, and attend live falconry shows. The castle is located near the village of Castelnaud-la-Chapelle, accessible via the D703 road.

c. Château les Merles (Address: Tuilières, 24520 Mouleydier, France):

Situated in the heart of the Dordogne countryside, Château les Merles offers elegant accommodations, gourmet dining, and an 18-hole golf course. Guests can relax by the outdoor pool, explore the surrounding vineyards, or take a leisurely bike ride along the nearby river. To reach the château, take the D21 road from Bergerac towards Mouleydier.

2. Hotels:

Dordogne boasts a wide range of hotels, ranging from boutique properties to budget-friendly options. Whether you're looking for a centrally located hotel in a bustling town or a secluded retreat in the countryside, you'll find plenty of choices to suit your needs. Here are three hotels worth considering:

a. Hôtel Plaza Madeleine (Address: 1 Place de la Petite Rigaudie, 24200 Sarlat-la-Canéda, France):

Located in the heart of Sarlat-la-Canéda, Hôtel Plaza Madeleine offers comfortable rooms, modern amenities, and easy access to the town's historic attractions and vibrant markets. Travelers on a budget can take advantage of special offers and packages available throughout the year.

b. Hôtel de Bouilhac (Address: 23 Rue de la République, 24200 Sarlat-la-Canéda, France):
Set within a beautifully restored 18th-century mansion, Hôtel de Bouilhac exudes old-world charm and elegance. Guests can relax in the hotel's peaceful courtyard, unwind in the cozy lounge area, or enjoy a delicious meal at the on-site restaurant.

c. Hôtel Mercure Bergerac Centre (Address: 2 Place Gambetta, 24100 Bergerac, France):
Ideally located in the heart of Bergerac, Hôtel Mercure Bergerac Centre offers stylish accommodations, modern facilities, and stunning views of the Dordogne River. Travelers can take advantage of the hotel's convenient location to explore the town's historic landmarks, charming streets, and bustling markets.

A map showing the various Château and boutique hotel accommodations nearby from the Bergerac Dordogne Périgord Airport

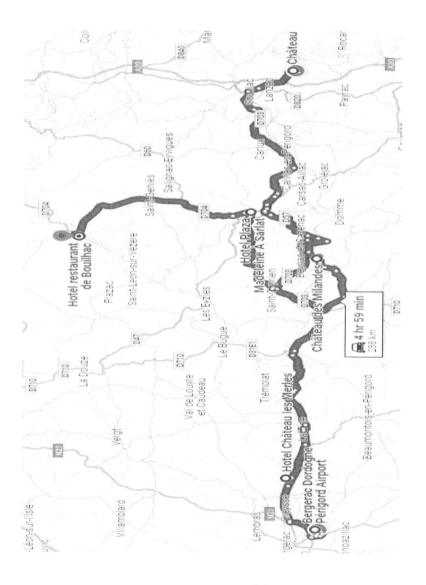

3. Bed & Breakfasts (Chambres d'Hôtes):

For travelers seeking a more intimate and personalized experience, bed and breakfasts (chambres d'hôtes) offer a warm welcome and a taste of local hospitality. Here are three charming B&Bs in Dordogne:

a. Le Moulin du Roc (Address: Avenue Eugène Le Roy, 24520 Champagnac-de-Belair, France):

Set within a historic 17th-century mill, Le Moulin du Roc offers cozy guest rooms, gourmet dining, and panoramic views of the Dronne River. Guests can relax in the tranquil gardens, explore the surrounding countryside, or sample local wines at nearby vineyards.

b. La Petite Clavelie (Address: La Petite Clavelie, 24510 Paussac-et-Saint-Vivien, France):

Tucked away in the peaceful countryside near Brantôme, La Petite Clavelie is a charming B&B housed within a renovated farmhouse. Guests can unwind in the comfortable guest rooms, enjoy a delicious homemade breakfast each morning, and explore the nearby villages, castles, and hiking trails.

c. Les Collines de Sainte Féréole (Address: Lieu-dit Sainte Féréole, 24290 Montignac, France):

Located just a short drive from the famous Lascaux caves, Les Collines de Sainte Féréole offers cozy guest rooms, a swimming pool, and stunning views of the surrounding countryside. Guests can start their day with a hearty breakfast featuring local produce before setting out to explore the region's prehistoric sites and natural wonders.

A map showing the various Bed & Breakfasts hotel accommodations nearby from the Bergerac Dordogne Périgord Airport

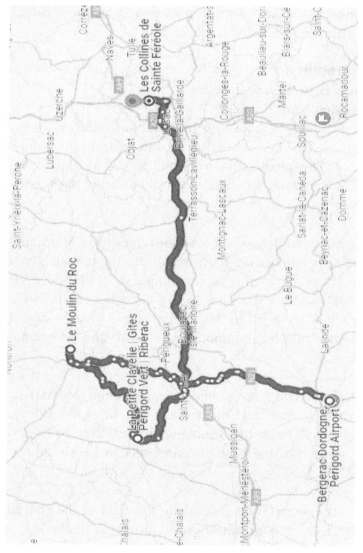

4. Gîtes:

Gîtes, or self-catering holiday homes, are a popular accommodation option in Dordogne, offering travelers the flexibility to explore the region at their own pace. Here are three charming gîtes worth considering:

a. Le Moulin de

Address: Le Moulin de la Beune
24200 Montignac France

Huddled along the banks of the tranquil Dordogne River, Le Moulin de la Beune exudes rustic charm and timeless elegance. This picturesque watermill turned boutique hotel is a hidden gem awaiting discovery in the heart of the Dordogne Valley.

Le Moulin de la Beune is conveniently located in Montignac, a quaint town known for its proximity to the famous Lascaux Caves. If you're traveling by car, simply input the address into your GPS or follow the signs to Montignac. Once you arrive in town, follow the signs to the hotel, which is situated along the riverbank, offering stunning views of the surrounding countryside.

For those relying on public transportation, Montignac is accessible by train and bus from major cities like Bordeaux and Limoges. From the Montignac train station or bus stop, it's a short taxi ride or a pleasant walk to Le Moulin de la Beune.

Upon arrival, you'll be greeted by the sight of the charming watermill, its wooden wheel gently turning in the breeze, and the soothing sound of the river flowing nearby. The hotel's serene ambiance and idyllic setting make it the perfect retreat for travelers seeking tranquility and natural beauty.

Whether you're lounging on the riverside terrace with a glass of local wine, exploring the nearby caves and historic sites, or simply unwinding in your cozy room adorned with traditional French décor, Le Moulin de la Beune offers an unforgettable experience in the heart of the Dordogne Valley.

Embrace the laid-back pace of life, immerse yourself in the region's rich history and culture, and let the enchanting atmosphere of Le Moulin de la Beune whisk you away on a journey of relaxation and discovery.

Dordogne on a budget

Exploring Dordogne on a budget is not only possible but can also be a richly rewarding experience. With a bit of planning and some insider tips, you can enjoy everything this beautiful region has to offer without breaking the bank.

1. Accommodation Options: Start by looking for affordable accommodation options. Dordogne has a wide range of budget-friendly places to stay, from charming bed and breakfasts to comfortable hostels and campgrounds. Websites like Booking.com and Airbnb can be useful for finding affordable stays. Consider staying in smaller towns or villages outside the main tourist areas for lower prices and a more authentic experience. For example, towns like Bergerac, Le Bugue, and Montignac offer lovely, cost-effective alternatives.

2. Getting There and Around: Traveling to Dordogne on a budget can be done by taking advantage of budget airlines flying into nearby airports like Bordeaux or Toulouse. From there, you can catch a train or bus to Dordogne. Look for discounted fares on sites like Skyscanner or Rome2Rio. Once in Dordogne, renting a bicycle or using local buses are economical ways to get around. Many towns are well-connected by bus services provided by companies like Transports en Commun de la Dordogne (TCD). For more flexibility, consider renting a small car; booking in advance can often yield significant savings.

3. Eating on a Budget: One of the joys of visiting Dordogne is sampling its culinary delights, and you can do this without spending a fortune. Visit local markets like Sarlat's Wednesday and Saturday markets to buy fresh produce, cheese, bread, and other local specialties. Picnic by the Dordogne River or in a picturesque village square for a memorable meal that won't cost much. Many bakeries (boulangeries) offer delicious, inexpensive sandwiches and pastries. When dining out, look for prix-fixe menus (set menus) offered by many restaurants, which provide a multi-course meal at a fixed price.

4. Affordable Attractions: Dordogne is packed with historical sites, natural beauty, and cultural experiences that can be enjoyed on a budget. Many castles and prehistoric sites offer reduced entry fees on certain days or for students and seniors. For instance, the Château de Beynac and the Grotte de Rouffignac have affordable entry prices.

Walking and hiking are free and provide some of the best ways to see the stunning landscapes. Explore trails like those around Les Eyzies or the Vézère Valley, where you can enjoy breathtaking views and historical sites. Additionally, many towns offer free walking tours that are both informative and enjoyable.

5. Free and Low-Cost Activities: There are plenty of free or low-cost activities in Dordogne. Visit the beautiful gardens of Marqueyssac, where entry is affordable, and on Thursday evenings during the summer, the gardens are illuminated by candlelight for a magical experience.

Attend local festivals and events, many of which are free to the public. The Summer Music Festival in Périgueux and the

Truffle Festival in Sarlat are wonderful cultural experiences that won't break the bank. Check local tourism websites for up-to-date information on events happening during your visit.

With these tips, you can experience the best of Dordogne without straining your wallet. Whether it's soaking up the region's rich history, indulging in local cuisine, or enjoying the stunning scenery, a budget-friendly trip to Dordogne can be incredibly fulfilling. Enjoy every moment of your adventure in this enchanting part of France..

What to Pack for Your Dordogne Adventure

Packing for a trip to Dordogne requires a bit of thought to ensure you are prepared for all the wonderful experiences that await you in this charming region. Here are a few recommendations on what to pack for your Dordogne trip, ensuring you have everything you need to make the most of your time.

1. Clothing Essentials: When packing clothes, consider the time of year you're visiting:

-   Spring and Autumn: These seasons can be quite variable, so bring layers. Pack lightweight sweaters, long-sleeve shirts, and a good waterproof jacket. A pair of comfortable jeans or trousers and a few t-shirts will serve you well.

- Summer: Summers in Dordogne can be warm, so bring light, breathable clothing like cotton shirts, shorts, and dresses. Don't forget a wide-brimmed hat, sunglasses, and a swimsuit for dips in the river or hotel pool.
- Winter: Winters are mild but can be chilly, especially in the mornings and evenings. Pack a warm coat, scarves, gloves, and layers like sweaters and thermal tops.

2.Footwear:Comfortable walking shoes are a must as you'll likely spend a lot of time exploring medieval villages and hiking trails. A sturdy pair of hiking boots will be invaluable if you plan on exploring the countryside or walking more rugged paths. Additionally, pack a pair of sandals or casual shoes for relaxing or dining out.

3. Accessories and Gear: Daypack: A small, comfortable backpack is perfect for carrying your daily essentials like water, snacks etc.

4. Documents and Money:
- Passport and ID: Ensure your passport is valid for the duration of your trip and keep a photocopy of it in a separate place as a backup.
- Travel Insurance: Having travel insurance can provide peace of mind in case of emergencies or unforeseen circumstances.
- Credit/Debit Cards and Cash:** While credit and debit cards are widely accepted, it's useful to have some euros in cash for small purchases or in places that might not accept cards.

5. Outdoor and Activity-Specific Gear: If you plan on engaging in specific activities, make sure to pack accordingly:
- Hiking Gear: Include a good pair of hiking boots, moisture-wicking socks, and a lightweight rain jacket. A hat and sunglasses are also essential.
- Water Activities:Bring a swimsuit, water shoes, and a quick-dry towel if you're planning on canoeing or kayaking.
- Cycling Gear: If you're planning to explore by bike, consider packing padded cycling shorts, a helmet, and a small repair kit.

Additional Tip
Pack Light: Dordogne is a region where you'll be moving around a lot, exploring different towns and attractions. Packing light will make your travels much easier.

By packing thoughtfully and efficiently, you'll be well-prepared to enjoy all that Dordogne has to offer. From the stunning landscapes and historic sites to the delicious food and welcoming people, having the right items with you will enhance your experience and allow you to focus on creating unforgettable memories.

Choosing the right tour package

In the enchanting realm of Dordogne, where medieval castles stand proud and vineyards stretch as far as the eye can see, selecting the ideal tour package can feel like finding the proverbial needle in a haystack. Fear not, fellow traveler, for with a discerning eye and a dash of insight, you'll uncover the perfect itinerary to unlock Dordogne's treasures. Here's how:

1. Define Your Dream Experience:
- Reflect on your travel aspirations. Are you drawn to the region's rich history, culinary delights, or outdoor adventures? Clarifying your preferences will guide you towards tour packages tailored to your interests.

2. Research, Research, Research:
- Dive into the depths of the internet and peruse travel websites, forums, and reviews to gather insights from fellow adventurers. Pay attention to tour operators with a track record of excellence and positive feedback from past travelers.

3. Seek Local Expertise:
- Tap into the wisdom of local tour operators and guides who possess intimate knowledge of Dordogne's hidden gems and cultural nuances. Their expertise can elevate your journey from ordinary to extraordinary.

4. Assess Inclusions and Exclusions:
- Scrutinize the details of each tour package, paying close attention to inclusions such as accommodations, meals, transportation, and guided excursions. Balance your budget

with the value offered by each package to ensure a rewarding investment.

5. Flexibility Is Key:
- Prioritize tour packages that offer flexibility and customization options, allowing you to tailor your itinerary to suit your preferences and pace. Embrace the spontaneity of travel and leave room for serendipitous discoveries along the way.

6. Consider Sustainability and Responsibility:
- Choose tour operators committed to sustainable and responsible travel practices, minimizing environmental impact and supporting local communities. Opt for experiences that promote cultural immersion and authentic interactions with residents.

7. Trust Your Intuition:
- Ultimately, trust your instincts when selecting a tour package. If a particular itinerary resonates with your soul and sparks excitement in your heart, chances are it's the perfect match for your Dordogne adventure.

With these guiding principles in mind, you're poised to navigate the labyrinth of tour packages and uncover the hidden treasures of Dordogne with confidence and anticipation. So choose wisely, dear traveler, and prepare to embark on a journey that will ignite your spirit and leave you enchanted by the wonders of Dordogne.

CHAPTER 2.

GETTING TO DORDOGNE:

Airports and Train stations

Embarking on your journey to Dordogne is the first step towards immersing yourself in the enchanting beauty and rich history of this picturesque region. Located in southwestern France, Dordogne beckons travelers with its rolling vineyards, medieval villages, and stunning landscapes. Getting to this idyllic destination is a breeze, whether you prefer the convenience of air travel, the romance of train journeys, or the flexibility of road trips.

For international travelers, the most common point of entry to Dordogne is through major airports such as Bordeaux-Mérignac Airport (BOD) and Bergerac Dordogne Périgord Airport (EGC). Both airports offer domestic and international flights, providing convenient access to the region. From Bordeaux-Mérignac Airport, located approximately 2.5 hours away by road, visitors can rent a car, hop on a train, or arrange for a private transfer to reach their final destination in Dordogne. Similarly, Bergerac Dordogne Périgord Airport, situated closer to the heart of Dordogne, offers car rental services and taxi options for onward travel.

Traveling by train is another popular option for reaching Dordogne, allowing travelers to sit back, relax, and admire the scenic beauty of the French countryside along the way. The TGV (Train à Grande Vitesse) high-speed train network connects major cities such as Paris, Bordeaux, and Toulouse to Dordogne, with stops at picturesque towns like Sarlat-la-Canéda and Périgueux. From these train stations, travelers can easily access local transportation options, including taxis, buses, and rental cars, to explore the surrounding area at their own pace.

For those who prefer the freedom of the open road, driving to Dordogne offers a sense of adventure and flexibility. France boasts an extensive network of well-maintained highways and scenic routes, making road trips a popular choice for travelers seeking to discover hidden gems off the beaten path. From Paris, the journey to Dordogne takes approximately 5-6 hours by car, passing through charming towns, vineyard-clad hillsides, and verdant countryside along the way. With plenty of rest stops, quaint cafes, and panoramic viewpoints to enjoy en route, the drive to Dordogne promises to be a memorable part of your travel experience.

No matter which mode of transportation you choose, arriving in Dordogne heralds the beginning of an unforgettable adventure. From the moment you set foot in this captivating region, you'll be greeted by the warm hospitality of its residents, the timeless beauty of its landscapes, and the tantalizing aromas of its world-renowned cuisine. So pack your bags, chart your course, and get ready to embark on a journey filled with discovery, exploration, and endless possibilities in Dordogne.

Choosing the Best flights

Choosing the best flights for your journey to Dordogne is a pivotal decision that can greatly influence the comfort, convenience, and overall enjoyment of your travel experience. With a myriad of options available, from budget airlines to premium carriers, finding the perfect flight requires careful consideration and strategic planning. Here's how to navigate the process and ensure a seamless journey to this enchanting region:

1. Start with Research: Begin your quest for the ideal flight by conducting thorough research on airlines that operate routes to Dordogne. Explore reputable travel websites and booking platforms to compare flight options, fares, and schedules. Pay attention to factors such as layover durations, departure and arrival times, and onboard amenities to narrow down your choices.

2. Consider Your Preferences: Take stock of your travel preferences and priorities. Are you willing to sacrifice convenience for cost savings, or do you prefer direct flights for maximum comfort and efficiency? Factor in considerations such as travel dates, flexibility, and personal comfort preferences when evaluating flight options.

3. Evaluate Airline Reputation: Assess the reputation and reliability of airlines serving your desired route to Dordogne. Look for reviews and feedback from past passengers regarding aspects such as customer service, punctuality, and overall satisfaction. Opt for airlines with a track record of safety,

professionalism, and positive passenger experiences to ensure a smooth journey from start to finish.

4. Compare Fare Options Compare fare options offered by different airlines to secure the best value for your money. Keep an eye out for special promotions, discounts, and package deals that may offer added perks or savings on your flight booking. Consider booking in advance or being flexible with your travel dates to take advantage of lower fares and promotional offers.

5. Check Baggage Policies: Review the baggage policies of airlines you're considering to avoid any surprises or hidden fees. Pay attention to restrictions on baggage size, weight, and number of allowable items, especially if you plan to travel with bulky or oversized luggage. Opt for airlines that offer generous baggage allowances and transparent pricing to minimize extra costs.

6. Look for Additional Amenities: Take into account the onboard amenities and services provided by airlines to enhance your travel experience. Consider factors such as seat comfort, in-flight entertainment options, meal offerings, and Wi-Fi connectivity when selecting your preferred airline. Choose airlines that prioritize passenger comfort and convenience to ensure a pleasant journey from takeoff to landing.

7. Book with Confidence: Once you've weighed your options and found the perfect flight, proceed with confidence and complete your booking with your chosen airline or travel

provider. Double-check your itinerary details, confirmations, and travel documents to ensure accuracy and peace of mind ahead of your journey to Dordogne.

By following these guidelines and taking a proactive approach to choosing the best flights for your trip to Dordogne, you can embark on your adventure with confidence, knowing that you've made informed decisions that prioritize your comfort, convenience, and overall satisfaction. So buckle up, sit back, and get ready to soar towards unforgettable experiences in this captivating corner of France.

Dordogne airport: Arrival and Orientation

Upon arriving at Dordogne airport, you'll be greeted by the rustic charm and tranquil atmosphere that characterize this captivating region of southwestern France. Huddled amidst rolling hills and verdant countryside, Dordogne airport serves as the gateway to an unforgettable adventure filled with medieval villages, lush vineyards, and cultural treasures waiting to be discovered.

As you step off the plane and breathe in the crisp, fresh air of Dordogne, take a moment to soak in the natural beauty and serene ambiance that surrounds you. Despite its modest size, Dordogne airport offers modern facilities and convenient amenities to ensure a smooth and hassle-free arrival experience for travelers.

Once inside the terminal, you'll find a range of services to assist you in navigating your way through the airport and onward to your destination. From baggage claim and car rental facilities to information desks staffed by friendly and knowledgeable personnel, Dordogne airport strives to provide travelers with everything they need to start their journey on the right foot.

For those in need of transportation to their final destination in Dordogne, several options are available, including taxis, shuttle services, and rental cars. Taxis are readily available outside the terminal building, offering a convenient and efficient way to reach your accommodation or explore the surrounding area. Alternatively, shuttle services can be pre-booked or arranged on-site, providing shared transportation to popular destinations within Dordogne.

If you prefer the freedom and flexibility of having your own vehicle, car rental agencies are conveniently located within the airport terminal, allowing you to pick up your rental car and hit the road in no time. With a rental car at your disposal, you'll have the freedom to explore Dordogne at your own pace, venturing off the beaten path to discover hidden gems and scenic viewpoints along the way.

As you embark on your Dordogne adventure, take a moment to orient yourself and familiarize yourself with the layout of the airport and surrounding area. Whether you're planning to delve into the region's rich history at medieval castles, indulge in gastronomic delights at local markets, or simply unwind amidst the picturesque landscapes of the countryside,

Dordogne airport serves as the perfect starting point for your exploration of this enchanting region.

With its warm hospitality, stunning natural scenery, and wealth of cultural treasures, Dordogne invites you to embark on a journey of discovery and adventure unlike any other. So embrace the spirit of exploration, immerse yourself in the charm of Dordogne, and prepare to create memories that will last a lifetime in this captivating corner of France.

Getting Around in Dordogne

Exploring the enchanting region of Dordogne requires thoughtful consideration of the various modes of transportation available. Whether you prefer the flexibility of a car, the eco-friendly appeal of cycling, the convenience of public transport, the leisurely pace of river travel, or the immersive experience of walking, Dordogne offers a range of options to suit your travel style. Here's a detailed guide on how to navigate Dordogne, complete with recommendations for transportation companies and tips to make your journey seamless and enjoyable.

1. By Car
Renting a car is the most versatile way to explore Dordogne, providing the freedom to visit remote villages, scenic spots, and historical sites at your own pace.
Recommendations and Tips
- Car Rental Companies: Major car rental agencies like Hertz, Avis, and Europcar have offices in Bergerac, Périgueux, and other key towns. Booking in advance can often secure better rates and vehicle availability.

- Navigation: Utilize GPS systems or apps like Google Maps or Waze to navigate the rural roads effectively.
- Parking: Towns such as Sarlat-la-Canéda offer public parking lots, though it's wise to arrive early, especially during peak tourist seasons.

2. By Bike
Cycling is a fantastic way to explore Dordogne's stunning landscapes and quaint villages. The region is well-suited for cyclists, with numerous scenic routes available.

Recommendations and Tips
- Bike Rental Services: Companies like BikeHireDirect and Aquitaine Bike offer a range of bicycles, including electric bikes, which are perfect for tackling Dordogne's hilly terrain.

- Cycling Maps: Obtain maps from local tourist offices or use apps like Komoot to plan your routes.

- Safety Gear: Always wear a helmet and be mindful of local traffic rules and road signs.

3. By Public Transport
Public transport is a cost-effective way to travel between major towns and some tourist attractions in Dordogne.

Recommendations:
- Trains: The regional TER trains connect larger towns such as Bergerac, Périgueux, and Sarlat-la-Canéda. SNCF operates these services, and tickets can be purchased online or at the station. Check schedules in advance as services can be infrequent.

- Buses: Local bus services operated by Transports Régionaux Nouvelle-Aquitaine connect various towns and villages. Routes and schedules can be found on their website or at local tourist offices.

- Taxis: For shorter trips or when public transport is not available, taxis are a convenient option. Companies like Taxi Dordogne and Allo Taxi Sarlat provide reliable services. Pre-booking is recommended, especially in rural areas.

4. By Boat
Exploring Dordogne by boat offers a serene and unique perspective of the region, especially along the Dordogne and Vézère rivers.

Recommendations and tips
- Boat Rentals: Companies like Canoe Vacances and Canoe Détente offer canoe and kayak rentals for both short trips and longer excursions. For a more leisurely experience, consider guided river cruises provided by Gabarres Norbert or Gabarres de Bergerac.

- Routes: Popular routes include the stretch between La Roque-Gageac and Beynac, known for its scenic beauty. Choose a route that matches your interest and skill level.

-Safety Gear: Life jackets are essential, and it's important to follow all safety instructions provided by rental services or tour operators.

On Foot
Walking is an excellent way to explore Dordogne's picturesque towns, historic sites, and beautiful countryside trails.

Recommendations and Tips
- Hiking Trails: The GR36 and local trails around towns like Domme and Les Eyzies offer varied landscapes and levels of difficulty. Detailed maps are available at tourist offices.

- Footwear: Wear comfortable and sturdy walking shoes suitable for different terrains.

- Guided Tours: For a deeper understanding of the area, consider joining a guided walking tour. Companies like Dordogne Experience and Perigord Walking Tours offer knowledgeable guides and well-planned routes.

Each mode of transportation in Dordogne has its own charm and benefits, catering to different preferences and travel styles. Whether you choose to drive, cycle, use public transport, travel by boat, or walk, you'll find that each offers a unique way to experience the beauty and history of this enchanting region. With this guide, you're well-equipped to make the most of your Dordogne adventure.

CHAPTER 3.
EXPLORING DORDOGNE
Major Cities and Towns

Exploring the major cities and towns of Dordogne is like stepping into a storybook, where medieval architecture, charming cobblestone streets, and bustling markets await around every corner. Each city and town in Dordogne possesses a distinct personality of its own and attractions, offering travelers a diverse range of experiences to enjoy.

Sarlat-la-Canéda:Medieval Marvel

Sarlat-la-Canéda is the crown jewel of Dordogne, a town that feels like stepping into a fairy tale. Its medieval charm, narrow winding streets, and golden stone buildings create a picturesque setting that captivates every visitor. As you walk through Sarlat, you can almost hear the whispers of history echoing from its ancient walls.

How to Get There
Getting to Sarlat-la-Canéda is quite straightforward. If you're flying in, the closest major airport is Bergerac Dordogne Périgord Airport, about an hour and a half away by car. From the airport, you can rent a car and take the D32 road, which will lead you directly to Sarlat. If you're coming by train, head to Sarlat Station, which is well-connected to major cities like Bordeaux and Toulouse. The train journey offers scenic views

of the French countryside, making it a delightful start to your adventure.

Exploring Sarlat

Once you arrive in Sarlat-la-Canéda, you'll be eager to dive into all it has to offer. Begin your journey at the heart of Sarlat, the Place de la Liberté. This lively square is surrounded by beautiful medieval buildings, each with its own story. The square is bustling with cafes and shops, making it a perfect spot to relax with a coffee and soak in the atmosphere.

Sitting in a quaint café at the Place de la Liberté, I sipped on a rich, aromatic coffee while watching the world go by. The friendly chatter of locals and the vibrant energy of the square made me feel like I was part of the community.

Also Visit the Sarlat Market, held every Wednesday and Saturday. Here, you can find local delicacies like truffles, foie gras, and walnut products. The vibrant stalls, filled with fresh produce, cheeses, and handmade crafts, provide an authentic taste of Dordogne.

The market was a feast for the senses. I wandered through the stalls, sampling creamy cheeses and fragrant truffle oils. A friendly vendor even taught me how to select the best foie gras, sharing stories of his family's culinary traditions.

A visit to Sarlat wouldn't be complete without exploring the Saint-Sacerdos Cathedral. Located at Place du Peyrou, this magnificent cathedral dates back to the 9th century and showcases stunning Gothic architecture. Inside, the serene ambiance and beautiful stained glass windows invite you to pause and reflect.

Stepping inside the cathedral, I was struck by its grandeur and tranquility. The light filtering through the stained glass created a kaleidoscope of colors, adding to the sacred atmosphere.

For the best view of Sarlat, climb the Bell Tower of Saint-Sacerdos Cathedral. The climb is a bit steep, but the panoramic views of the town and surrounding countryside are well worth the effort. On a clear day, the sight is truly breathtaking. Reaching the top of the bell tower, I was greeted by a stunning vista. The entire town of Sarlat spread out below me, with its golden stone buildings and winding streets. It was a moment of pure awe and wonder.

Take a leisurely stroll down Rue de la République, Sarlat's main street. This pedestrian-friendly road is lined with charming shops, bakeries, and cafes. Pop into a patisserie for a fresh croissant or browse the boutiques for unique souvenirs. Strolling down Rue de la République, I found a delightful patisserie. The scent of freshly baked pastries drew me in, and I couldn't resist trying a buttery croissant. It was the perfect treat as I continued exploring.

If you're visiting in summer, the Sarlat Theatre Festival is a must-see. Held in July and August, this festival transforms the town into a stage, with performances ranging from classical plays to modern interpretations. The festival's lively atmosphere adds a vibrant touch to your visit. Watching a play under the stars during the Sarlat Theatre Festival was magical. The performances were captivating, and the audience's enthusiasm was infectious. It felt like the entire town came together to celebrate art and culture.

Sarlat is a paradise for food lovers. Enjoy a meal at L'Adresse (Address: 12 Rue Fénelon, 24200 Sarlat-la-Canéda, France where you can savor traditional Dordogne cuisine in a cozy setting. For a more upscale experience, try Le Grand Bleu (Address: 43 Avenue de la Gare, 24200 Sarlat-la-Canéda, France; Phone: +33 5 53 31 08 48), a Michelin-starred restaurant known for its innovative dishes and impeccable service. Dining at Le Grand Bleu was an unforgettable experience. The creative dishes were a feast for both the eyes and the palate, and the impeccable service made the evening truly special.

End your day with a peaceful walk in the Jardin des Enfeus, a tranquil garden located next to the Saint-Sacerdos Cathedral. The garden's serene environment, with its ancient tombs and beautiful greenery, provides a perfect escape from the bustling town center. Strolling through Jardin des Enfeus, I found a quiet bench and sat down to absorb the tranquility. The sound of birds singing and the gentle rustle of leaves created a calming atmosphere, making it a perfect spot to unwind.

Accommodation For a comfortable stay, consider Hôtel de Selves (Address: 93 Avenue de Selves, 24200 Sarlat-la-Canéda, France; offering modern amenities and a convenient location. If you prefer a more rustic charm, La Villa des Consuls (Address: 3 Rue Jean Jacques Rousseau, 24200

Sarlat-la-Canéda, France, provides beautifully decorated rooms in a historic setting.

Sarlat-la-Canéda is not just a destination; it's an experience that stays with you long after you leave. From its rich history and stunning architecture to its vibrant markets and delicious cuisine, Sarlat offers a perfect blend of cultural immersion and relaxation. Whether you're wandering its cobbled streets or enjoying a meal at a local restaurant, every moment in Sarlat is a step back in time, wrapped in the warm embrace of French hospitality.

Bergerac

Bergerac is a delightful town nestled along the banks of the Dordogne River, known for its rich history, charming old town, and world-renowned wines. The town exudes a quintessentially French ambiance with its medieval architecture, picturesque squares, and the ever-present allure of vineyards. Exploring Bergerac is like taking a step back in time while enjoying the modern comforts and pleasures that make it an exceptional travel destination.

How to Get There
Reaching Bergerac is convenient whether you're arriving by air, train, or car. Bergerac Dordogne Périgord Airport is just a few kilometers from the town center, making it an ideal entry point. From the airport, you can take a taxi or rent a car to reach the town within 15 minutes. If you prefer the train, Bergerac has a well-connected train station with regular services from Bordeaux and Sarlat. Driving is also a scenic

option, with the D936 and N21 roads offering beautiful views of the French countryside as you approach the town.

Exploring Bergerac

Once in Bergerac, you'll find plenty to see and do. Here are some highlights to ensure you make the most of your visit.

1. Wander the Old Town: Begin your exploration in the historic heart of Bergerac. The old town, with its narrow, cobbled streets and half-timbered houses, is perfect for a leisurely stroll. The main square, Place Pelissière, is a charming spot lined with cafes and shops. Here, you can enjoy a coffee or a glass of local wine while soaking up the atmosphere. Walking through the old town, I was enchanted by the medieval architecture and vibrant flowers adorning the buildings. Every corner seemed to hold a new surprise, from quaint boutiques to inviting patisseries.

2. Visit the Cyrano de Bergerac Statue: A visit to Bergerac wouldn't be complete without paying homage to its most famous fictional resident, Cyrano de Bergerac. There are two statues of Cyrano in the town, one in Place Pelissière and another near the Old Port. These statues celebrate the literary character who, although never actually lived in Bergerac, has become a symbol of the town. Seeing the Cyrano de Bergerac statue in Place Pelissière was a delightful moment. Surrounded by the charm of the old town, the statue added a whimsical touch to my visit.

3. Explore the Wine Museum: Bergerac is renowned for its wines, and the Maison des Vins de Bergerac (Address: 1 Rue

des Récollets, 24100 Bergerac, France) is the perfect place to learn about them. Housed in a beautiful 17th-century cloister, the museum offers an immersive experience into the region's winemaking history and traditions. Don't miss the opportunity to taste some of the finest local wines in their tasting room.

The wine museum was a highlight of my trip. I learned so much about the local wine production and enjoyed a tasting session that introduced me to some exquisite Bergerac wines.

4. Take a River Cruise: One of the best ways to appreciate Bergerac's scenic beauty is by taking a river cruise on the Dordogne River. These cruises offer a unique perspective of the town and its surrounding landscapes. Companies like Gabarres de Bergerac (Address: Quai Salvette, 24100 Bergerac, France) offer various cruise options, from short tours to longer excursions.

The river cruise was a serene and picturesque experience. Gliding along the Dordogne River, I enjoyed stunning views of the town and countryside, making it a truly memorable part of my visit.

5. Visit the Tobacco Museum: For something a bit different, the Musée du Tabac (Address: Maison Peyrarède, Place du Feu, 24100 Bergerac, France;) offers an intriguing look at the history of tobacco in the region. The museum is located in a beautiful 17th-century building and features a fascinating collection of artifacts related to the cultivation and use of tobacco. The Tobacco Museum provided a unique insight into

a lesser-known aspect of Bergerac's history. The exhibits were well-curated and offered a fascinating glimpse into the past.

7. Relax in the Gardens: Bergerac has several lovely gardens perfect for a leisurely afternoon. The Cloître des Récollets garden, located next to the Maison des Vins, offers a peaceful retreat with its well-maintained flower beds and historical charm. Another great spot is the Parc de Pombonne, a bit further from the town center but worth the visit for its natural beauty and tranquil ambiance. Taking a stroll in the Cloître des Récollets garden was a soothing experience. The well-manicured flower beds and the peaceful atmosphere made it a perfect place to unwind.

Accommodation
For a comfortable stay, consider Hôtel de Bordeaux (Address: 38 Place Gambetta, 24100 Bergerac, France), which offers a blend of modern amenities and classic charm. Another great option is La Chartreuse du Bignac (Address: Le Bignac, 24520 Saint-Nexans, France), a luxurious countryside retreat located just outside Bergerac, providing a serene and picturesque setting.

Bergerac is a destination that perfectly blends history, culture, and natural beauty. From its charming old town and iconic statues to its delightful wine experiences and scenic river cruises, Bergerac offers a wealth of activities that cater to every traveler's interests. Whether you're a history buff, a wine enthusiast, or simply looking for a picturesque place to relax, Bergerac has something special to offer.

Périgueux

Welcome to Périgueux, the vibrant capital of the Dordogne department. With its blend of ancient history, cultural heritage, and modern amenities, Périgueux offers a captivating experience for visitors of all interests.

How to Get There

Périgueux is conveniently located in the heart of the Dordogne region, making it easily accessible by various modes of transportation. If you're arriving by train, Périgueux has its own train station, with regular services connecting it to major cities like Bordeaux and Limoges. If you prefer driving, the town is accessible via the A89 motorway, which links it to major routes across France. Alternatively, you can fly into Bergerac Dordogne Périgord Airport and take a scenic drive to Périgueux.

Exploring Périgueux

Once you arrive in Périgueux, you'll be enchanted by its historic charm, architectural wonders, and lively ambiance. Here are some highlights to help you make the most of your visit:

1. Discover the Old Town:Begin your exploration in the Old Town (Vieux Périgueux), where history comes to life amidst narrow cobblestone streets and ancient buildings. Admire the stunning Romanesque architecture of the Saint-Front Cathedral, a UNESCO World Heritage Site, and wander

through the charming squares and alleys lined with boutiques, cafes, and galleries.

2. Explore the Périgueux Cathedral: The Saint-Front Cathedral is a masterpiece of Romanesque architecture and a symbol of Périgueux's rich heritage. Step inside this majestic cathedral to marvel at its soaring vaulted ceilings, intricate carvings, and beautiful stained glass windows. Climb the bell tower for panoramic views of the town and surrounding countryside.

3. Visit the Vesunna Gallo-Roman Museum: Delve into Périgueux's ancient past at the Vesunna Gallo-Roman Museum, located on the site of a former Roman villa. Explore the museum's fascinating exhibits, which showcase artifacts from the Roman settlement of Vesunna, including mosaics, sculptures, and everyday objects. Don't miss the chance to walk through the remains of the villa's thermal baths, where you can glimpse life in Roman times.

4. Wander Through the Périgueux Market: Experience the vibrant atmosphere of the Périgueux market, held every Wednesday and Saturday in the historic town center. Browse stalls overflowing with fresh produce, regional delicacies, and artisanal crafts, and soak up the sights, sounds, and smells of this bustling market. Be sure to sample local specialties like foie gras, truffles, and walnut products.

5. Relax in Jardin des Arènes: Take a leisurely stroll through Jardin des Arènes, a peaceful oasis nestled in the heart of Périgueux. Admire the lush greenery, fragrant flowers, and

ancient ruins that dot the landscape, and find a quiet spot to relax and enjoy a picnic or simply soak up the sunshine.

Accommodation

For a comfortable stay in Périgueux, consider Hotel Mercure Périgueux Centre (Address: 7 Place Francheville, 24000 Périgueux, France), a modern hotel with stylish accommodations and convenient amenities.

Périgueux is a captivating destination that offers a perfect blend of history, culture, and natural beauty. Whether you're exploring its ancient landmarks, savoring its culinary delights, or simply soaking up the ambiance of its charming streets, Périgueux promises an unforgettable experience that will leave you longing to return. So pack your bags and prepare to embark on a journey of discovery in this enchanting corner of France.

Domme

Domme, a picturesque hilltop village perched high above the Dordogne River. With its stunning views, medieval architecture, and rich history, it offers a unique and unforgettable experience for visitors. Here are some highlights to help you make the most of your visit:

How to Get There

Domme is located in the heart of the Dordogne region and can be reached by various means of transportation. If you're driving, take the D46 road from Sarlat-la-Canéda, which will lead you directly to the village. Alternatively, you can take a scenic boat cruise along the Dordogne River, offering breathtaking views of Domme and its surrounding countryside.

Exploring Domme

Once you arrive in Domme, you'll be captivated by its charming streets, ancient ramparts, and panoramic vistas. As you wander through the cobblestone streets of Domme's Old Town, you'll feel like you've stepped back in time. I was enchanted by the medieval architecture and the sense of history that permeates every corner of the village. Don't miss the chance to explore the hidden squares and alleyways, where you'll discover quaint shops, artisanal boutiques, and cozy cafes.

Visit the Place de la Halle: The Place de la Halle is the beating heart of Domme, a lively square where locals and visitors alike gather to enjoy the vibrant atmosphere. I spent an afternoon sipping coffee at one of the outdoor terraces, watching the world go by and soaking in the charm of this picturesque village square.

Explore the Domme Caves: Descending into the depths of the Domme Caves was a highlight of my visit. Guided by a knowledgeable tour guide, I marveled at the intricate rock formations, underground rivers, and hidden chambers that lay hidden beneath the surface. It was a truly unforgettable experience that gave me a newfound appreciation for the geological wonders of the region.

Admire the Panoramic Views: The Belvédère de la Barre offers some of the most breathtaking views in the Dordogne Valley, and it's not hard to see why. Standing on the edge of the cliff, I was awe-struck by the sweeping vistas of the surrounding countryside, with the meandering Dordogne River winding its way through the landscape below. It was a moment of pure tranquility and beauty that will stay with me forever.

No visit to Domme would be complete without sampling the local cuisine. I treated myself to a delicious meal at one of the village's cozy restaurants, where I indulged in regional specialties like foie gras, truffles, and walnut cake. The flavors were exquisite, and the warm hospitality of the locals made the experience even more memorable.

Accommodation

For a truly memorable stay in Domme, I highly recommend booking a room at La Perle de Domme (Address; 571 Taire du Grel, 24250 Domme, France) or Le Relais de la Moussidière. Situated in Sarlat-la-Canéda, which is about a 20-minute drive from Domme. This charming hotel offers comfortable accommodations and stunning views of the surrounding countryside. The friendly staff and cozy atmosphere made me feel right at home, and I can't wait to return someday.

Domme is a hidden gem of the Dordogne region, offering a perfect blend of history, culture, and natural beauty. Whether you're exploring its medieval streets, admiring its panoramic views, or indulging in its culinary delights, Domme promises an unforgettable experience that will linger in your memories long after you've left. So come and discover the enchantment of Domme for yourself – you won't be disappointed.

Les Eyzies-de-Tayac-Sireuil

Les Eyzies-de-Tayac-Sireuil, often referred to simply as Les Eyzies. This charming village is the world capital of prehistory, boasting a rich tapestry of archaeological sites, prehistoric caves, and fascinating museums. Located in the heart of the Vézère Valley, Les Eyzies offers an unparalleled glimpse into our ancient past.

How to Get There

Les Eyzies is accessible by car, train, or bus. If you're driving, it's about a 45-minute drive from Sarlat-la-Canéda via the D47 road. For those relying on public transportation, the village has its own train station, Les Eyzies, with regular services from Bordeaux and Périgueux. Buses also connect Les Eyzies with other towns in the Dordogne region, making it easy to include in your itinerary.

Exploring Les Eyzies

Les Eyzies is a treasure trove of prehistoric marvels and natural beauty. Here's how to make the most of your visit:

1. Discover the National Museum of Prehistory: Start your journey at the National Museum of Prehistory (Musée National de Préhistoire). Located in the heart of the village, this museum houses one of the world's most extensive collections of prehistoric artifacts. As you wander through the

exhibits, you'll encounter tools, bones, and art objects that tell the story of early human life in the Vézère Valley. The museum provides a comprehensive introduction to the region's prehistoric heritage.

2. Visit the Font-de-Gaume Cave: One of the few remaining caves in France with polychrome prehistoric paintings still open to the public, Font-de-Gaume is a must-visit. The cave features stunning animal depictions, including bison, horses, and mammoths, painted over 17,000 years ago. Due to its fragility, visitor numbers are limited, so it's essential to book your tour in advance.

3. Explore the Grotte des Combarelles: Another remarkable site is the Grotte des Combarelles, renowned for its intricate engravings dating back to the Magdalenian period. The cave walls are adorned with more than 600 engravings of animals and symbols, offering a unique insight into prehistoric art and culture. Like Font-de-Gaume, visits are limited and booking ahead is crucial.

4. Marvel at the Abri de Cro-Magnon: Located near the village, the Abri de Cro-Magnon is the famous rock shelter where the first remains of Cro-Magnon man were discovered in 1868. The site includes a small museum with exhibits that provide context and background on the discovery and significance of Cro-Magnon humans.

5. Stroll Through the Village: Les Eyzies itself is a picturesque village with charming stone houses, quaint shops, and delightful cafes. Take a leisurely stroll through its streets, and

enjoy the serene atmosphere and stunning natural scenery. Don't miss the chance to sample local delicacies at one of the village's restaurants, where you can enjoy regional dishes such as confit de canard and walnut cake.

Accommodation: After a day of exploration, rest in one of Les Eyzies' cozy accommodations. For a touch of luxury, consider staying at Hôtel Les Glycines (Address: 4 Avenue de Laugerie, 24620 Les Eyzies-de-Tayac-Sireuil, France; Phone: +33 5 53 06 97 07). This elegant hotel offers modern amenities, beautiful gardens, and a gourmet restaurant.

Les Eyzies-de-Tayac-Sireuil is a journey back in time, offering a unique and enriching experience for anyone fascinated by prehistory. From its world-class museums to its awe-inspiring caves, this village invites you to uncover the secrets of our ancient ancestors. So, dear traveler, let Les Eyzies enchant you with its history and beauty, and make your visit an unforgettable adventure.

A map showing major cities and towns from Bergerac Airport to Sarlat-la-Canéda, Périgueux, Domme, Les Eyzies-de-Tayac-Sireuil

CHAPTER 4:
HISTORIC AND CULTURAL SITES

Dordogne is equally remarkable for its wealth of historic and cultural sites that tell the stories of bygone eras. From ancient caves adorned with prehistoric art to majestic castles that have stood the test of time.

Imagine standing in the Lascaux Caves, marveling at paintings created thousands of years ago, or walking through the grand halls of Château de Beynac, feeling the echoes of medieval knights and nobles. These experiences aren't just about seeing the sights; they are about connecting with the stories and lives of those who came before us.

In this chapter, we'll explore these iconic locations and more. Each site we visit offers a unique glimpse into Dordogne's rich heritage, with personal insights and recommendations to help you make the most of your visit. Whether you're a history enthusiast, an art lover, or simply curious about the past, this chapter will guide you through the best historic and cultural gems of Dordogne. Join me on this journey to uncover the stories and secrets that make this region so special

The Castles of Dordogne

Welcome to the enchanting world of Dordogne's castles, where history comes alive through majestic stone walls and panoramic views. The Dordogne region, also known as Périgord, is home to over a thousand castles, each with its own unique story and charm. These castles are not just relics of the past; they are vibrant, living pieces of history that invite you to step back in time and imagine the lives of those who once walked their halls.

1. Château de Beynac

Address: Château de Beynac, 24220 Beynac-et-Cazenac, France.

Château de Beynac is located in the village of Beynac-et-Cazenac. From Sarlat-la-Canéda, take the D703 road west for about 10 kilometers. Signs for the château will guide you the rest of the way.

When you arrive at Château de Beynac, the first thing you'll notice is its dramatic position perched high on a cliff overlooking the Dordogne River. The view alone is worth the visit. As you walk through the castle, you'll be struck by the well-preserved medieval architecture. Climbing up the spiral staircases and wandering through the great halls, I could almost hear the clanking of knights' armor and the whisper of courtly intrigue.

Make sure to visit the castle's battlements. Standing there, I felt like a lord surveying my domain, with the lush Dordogne Valley stretching out below me. The sense of history is palpable, and the guided tours provide fascinating insights into the castle's role in the Hundred Years' War and its eventual restoration.

2. Château des Milandes

Address: Château des Milandes, 24250 Castelnaud-la-Chapelle, France.

Château des Milandes is situated near Castelnaud-la-Chapelle. From Sarlat-la-Canéda, head south on the D57 for about 20 kilometers.

Château des Milandes is perhaps best known as the former home of the famous singer and actress Josephine Baker. As you explore the beautiful Renaissance-style château, you'll learn about Baker's incredible life and her efforts during World War II. Walking through the rooms filled with her memorabilia, I felt inspired by her courage and charisma.

The château also boasts stunning gardens. Strolling through the perfectly manicured hedges and vibrant flowerbeds, I took a moment to relax by the fountains and soak in the serene atmosphere. Don't miss the bird of prey show – watching the majestic eagles and hawks soar above the castle grounds was a highlight of my visit.

3. Château de Castelnaud
Address: Château de Castelnaud, 24250 Castelnaud-la-Chapelle, France.

Château de Castelnaud is located in the village of Castelnaud-la-Chapelle. From Sarlat-la-Canéda, take the D57 south for about 15 kilometers.

Château de Castelnaud is a must-visit for anyone interested in medieval warfare. The castle houses an impressive collection of arms and armor, and the exhibits are well-presented and informative. As I wandered through the museum, I was fascinated by the displays of swords, crossbows, and full suits of armor.

One of the most exciting parts of my visit was seeing the live demonstrations of medieval weapons. Watching a trebuchet in action was thrilling, and it gave me a real appreciation for the engineering skills of the past. The views from the castle ramparts are spectacular, offering a perfect spot for photography enthusiasts.

4. Château de Commarque

Address: Château de Commarque, 24620 Les Eyzies-de-Tayac-Sireuil, France.

Château de Commarque is located near the town of Les Eyzies-de-Tayac-Sireuil. From Sarlat-la-Canéda, drive northeast on the D47 for about 18 kilometers.

Exploring Château de Commarque was like stepping into a fairy tale. The castle is partially in ruins, which only adds to its mystique and charm. As I climbed the ancient stone steps and wandered through the crumbling towers, I felt like an adventurer uncovering hidden secrets from centuries past.

The site is nestled in a lush, green valley, making it perfect for a peaceful walk or a picnic. I took some time to explore the surrounding woods and caves, where prehistoric carvings can still be seen. The blend of natural beauty and historical intrigue at Commarque is truly unique and unforgettable.

The castles of Dordogne are more than just tourist attractions; they are windows into the region's rich and tumultuous history. Each castle has its own story, and visiting them is like taking a journey through time. From the grandeur of Château de Beynac to the personal history of Château des Milandes, these sites offer something for everyone.

As you explore these incredible landmarks, take your time to soak in the atmosphere, imagine the lives of those who once lived there, and appreciate the stunning landscapes that surround them. Dordogne's castles are waiting to share their stories with you – all you need to do is listen.

Lascaux Caves and Prehistoric Art

The Lascaux Caves, often referred to as the "Sistine Chapel of Prehistory," are a must-visit for anyone traveling to Dordogne. These caves, located near the village of Montignac, are home to some of the most remarkable prehistoric art ever discovered. The paintings, estimated to be around 17,000 years old, offer a window into the lives and imaginations of our ancient ancestors.

To get to Lascaux Caves, take the D704 from Sarlat-la-Canéda and drive northeast for about 25 kilometers until you reach Montignac. Clear signs will guide you to the site from the town.

Upon arriving at Lascaux IV, the International Centre for Cave Art, you'll be amazed by the modern architecture designed to blend seamlessly with the surrounding landscape. The center offers a state-of-the-art replica of the original Lascaux Cave, allowing visitors to experience the wonder of these ancient artworks without damaging the fragile originals.

As I stepped into the cool, dimly lit replica cave, I felt a sense of awe and reverence. The paintings of horses, bulls, deer, and other animals are incredibly detailed and vibrant, despite their age. The artistry and skill displayed by these early humans are truly remarkable. The tour guide explained the significance of the different scenes and how they might have been created using natural pigments and rudimentary tools. This experience made me appreciate the ingenuity and creativity of our distant ancestors.

In addition to the cave replica, the center features interactive exhibits and virtual reality experiences that delve deeper into the world of prehistoric art. These exhibits help to contextualize the paintings within the broader scope of human history and evolution. I spent hours exploring these displays, each one offering new insights and sparking my curiosity.

Outside the main building, the surrounding countryside of Montignac is perfect for a leisurely walk. The lush greenery and tranquil setting provide a stark contrast to the bustling cave center, offering a moment to reflect on the incredible journey back in time that you've just experienced.

Visiting Lascaux IV was a truly moving experience. As I stood in front of the magnificent Great Hall of the Bulls, I couldn't help but feel a deep connection to the people who created these artworks thousands of years ago. It's one thing to read about prehistoric art in books or see pictures online, but being there in person brings a profound sense of wonder and respect for our shared human heritage.

One of the highlights of my visit was the virtual reality tour that allowed me to explore parts of the original cave that are no longer accessible to the public. This immersive experience made me feel as though I was stepping into the past, walking alongside the ancient artists as they brought their visions to life on the cave walls.

After my tour, I sat down at the on-site café, sipping a coffee and contemplating the sheer magnitude of what I had just seen. The serene environment and the incredible art I had witnessed left a lasting impression on me, making Lascaux one of the most memorable parts of my trip to Dordogne.

Address: Lascaux IV International Centre for Cave Art, Avenue de Lascaux, 24290 Montignac, France.

Recommendations

- Guided Tours:Opt for a guided tour to get the most out of your visit. The guides are knowledgeable and passionate, providing context and stories that bring the cave art to life.
- Virtual Reality Experience: Don't miss the virtual reality tour. It's a unique way to explore the caves and understand the scale and detail of the artwork.

- Interactive Exhibits: Spend time with the interactive exhibits at Lascaux IV. They are engaging and educational, perfect for visitors of all ages.

- Timing Your Visit: Try to visit early in the morning or later in the afternoon to avoid the busiest times and enjoy a more relaxed experience.

-Nearby Attractions: While in Montignac, take the opportunity to explore the charming village and its surroundings. The picturesque streets and local shops add to the overall experience of your trip.

The Lascaux Caves and the International Centre for Cave Art offer an unforgettable journey into our prehistoric past. The detailed paintings, immersive experiences, and educational exhibits provide a comprehensive understanding of this remarkable period in human history. Whether you're a history buff, an art enthusiast, or simply curious about our ancestors, a visit to Lascaux is an essential part of any trip to Dordogne. Let the ancient art inspire you and leave you with a deeper appreciation for the creativity and ingenuity of early humans.

Museums and Galleries

Settled amidst the rolling hills and picturesque villages of Dordogne, lie hidden treasures waiting to be discovered within its museums and galleries. From prehistoric artifacts to contemporary art, there's something to captivate every visitor's imagination.

One such gem is the Musée National de Préhistoire, located at 1 rue du musée, 24620 Les Eyzies-de-Tayac. To get there, visitors can take a scenic drive through the Dordogne countryside or use public transportation, with Les Eyzies-de-Tayac served by a local bus network. The museum is open daily from 10 am to 6 pm (closed on Tuesdays). Admission is paid, but the insights gained are priceless.

For art enthusiasts, a visit to the **Musée d'Art et d'Archéologie du Périgord** in Périgueux is a must. Situated at 22 Cours Tourny, 24000 Périgueux, the museum is easily accessible by car or public transportation, with the Périgueux train station located nearby. The museum is open from 9 am to 12:30 pm and 2 pm to 5:30 pm (closed on Tuesdays). Entrance is paid, but the artistic inspiration gained is invaluable.

In the heart of Sarlat-la-Canéda lies the **Maison de la Boétie**, located at 37 rue de la Boétie, 24200 Sarlat-la-Canéda. Visitors can reach the museum on foot from the town center or by using local transportation options. The museum is open daily from 10 am to 12:30 pm and 2 pm to 6 pm (closed on Mondays). Entrance is free, making it an accessible destination for history buffs and curious minds alike.

To make the most of your time at these museums and galleries, consider joining a guided tour or participating in a workshop or lecture. Many establishments offer educational programs and special events designed to enhance the visitor experience and deepen your understanding of the exhibits. Additionally, don't forget to take your time wandering through the halls, soaking in the beauty of the artworks and artifacts, and allowing yourself to be transported through time and space by the stories they tell.

Whether you're a history buff, an art aficionado, or simply a curious traveler eager to explore new horizons, Dordogne's museums and galleries offer a wealth of experiences waiting to be discovered. So, pack your bags, open your mind, and prepare for a journey through the rich tapestry of human history and creativity that awaits you in this enchanting corner of France.

A Map of Historic and Cultural Sites showcasing the journey from the Lascaux Caves to the various museums and galleries recommended in this guide.

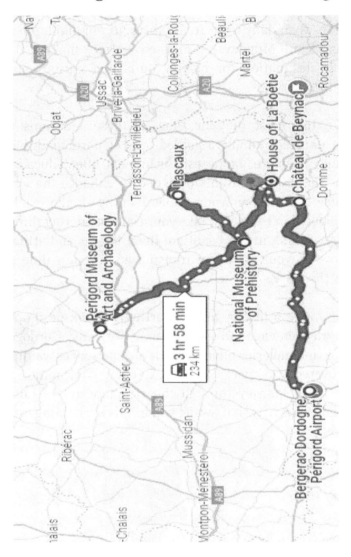

Rocamadour:pilgrimage and Panorama

Situated high on a cliffside, Rocamadour is one of the most breathtaking and spiritually significant destinations in the Dordogne region. This medieval village has been a key pilgrimage site for centuries, drawing visitors with its dramatic setting, historic structures, and deep sense of reverence.

To reach Rocamadour, drive along the D704 from Sarlat-la-Canéda, heading southeast. The journey is about 50 kilometers and takes around an hour by car. Alternatively, you can take a train to Rocamadour-Padirac station and then a short taxi ride or shuttle to the village.

As I first approached Rocamadour, the sight of the village cascading down the sheer cliff face took my breath away. It was like stepping into a scene from a fantasy novel, with ancient stone buildings seemingly clinging to the rock, topped by the majestic sanctuary of Notre-Dame.

Explore the Sanctuary of Notre-Dame: The sanctuary complex is the heart of Rocamadour and includes the famous Chapelle Notre-Dame, home to the Black Madonna, a revered statue that has drawn pilgrims for centuries. As I climbed the Grand Staircase, a path trodden by countless pilgrims, I felt a profound sense of connection to the history and spirituality of this place. Inside the chapel, the serene atmosphere and the soft glow of candlelight around the Black Madonna created a moment of quiet reflection and awe.

Next, I visited the Basilica of Saint-Sauveur, a UNESCO World Heritage site. The architecture is stunning, with its Gothic and

Romanesque elements. The adjacent Crypt of Saint Amadour, where the relics of the saint are kept, added to the sense of mystique and history. Walking through these sacred spaces, I was struck by the devotion and artistry that has preserved them through the ages.

After exploring the religious sites, I wandered through Rocamadour's narrow, winding streets. The village is full of quaint shops selling local crafts, religious souvenirs, and regional delicacies. I couldn't resist stopping at a small café for a taste of Rocamadour cheese, a creamy goat cheese that is one of the area's specialties. The flavor was rich and tangy, a perfect complement to the rustic bread and local wine.

Visit the Château: Perched atop the cliff, the Château de Rocamadour offers stunning panoramic views of the Alzou Valley. A short climb from the village leads to the castle, and the effort is well worth it. As I stood on the ramparts, looking out over the verdant landscape, I felt a deep sense of peace and perspective. The beauty of the Dordogne countryside stretched out before me, a patchwork of fields, forests, and distant hills.

The Monkey Forest and the Eagle Rock: For a change of pace, I decided to visit the nearby attractions of the Forêt des Singes (Monkey Forest) and the Rocher des Aigles (Eagle Rock). At the Monkey Forest, I walked among free-roaming Barbary macaques, observing their playful interactions and learning about their conservation. The Eagle Rock offered an impressive display of birds of prey, including eagles, vultures, and falcons. Watching these majestic birds soar against the backdrop of the cliffs was a thrilling experience.

Rocamadour is a place where history, spirituality, and natural beauty converge to create an unforgettable experience. Whether you're exploring the ancient sanctuaries, savoring local delicacies, or simply soaking in the breathtaking views, Rocamadour offers a unique and deeply enriching journey. Let the timeless charm and profound serenity of this cliffside village leave an indelible mark on your heart, as it did on mine. Address: Rocamadour, 46500, France.

Abbeys and Churches

The Dordogne region is home to a wealth of historic abbeys and churches, each telling a story of faith, artistry, and resilience. These sacred sites, with their stunning architecture and serene atmospheres, provide a glimpse into the spiritual and cultural history of the region.

The abbeys and churches in Dordogne are spread across the region, often nestled in picturesque villages or secluded countryside spots. To fully appreciate these sites, having a car is ideal for exploring at your own pace. Many of the locations are accessible via well-maintained roads and are signposted from major towns.

1. Abbey of Cadouin
Address: Place de l'Abbaye, 24480 Cadouin, France.

The Abbey of Cadouin is a Cistercian monastery founded in 1115, renowned for its stunning Gothic cloister. As I walked through the abbey's tranquil grounds, I was struck by the sense of peace and reverence that pervaded the site. The intricate stone carvings and detailed sculptures of the cloister were particularly captivating, offering a window into the craftsmanship of medieval artisans. The abbey also houses a museum that chronicles its history and the famous Holy Shroud that once drew pilgrims from across Europe.

2. Saint-Front Cathedral in Périgueux
Address: Place de la Clautre, 24000 Périgueux, France.

Dominating the skyline of Périgueux, the Saint-Front Cathedral is an architectural marvel with its unique Byzantine and Romanesque design. Walking into the cathedral, I was immediately struck by the grandeur of its domes and the serenity of its interior. The cathedral's layout, inspired by St. Mark's Basilica in Venice, adds to its distinctive charm. Climbing to the upper levels provided a panoramic view of Périgueux, a sight that made the visit even more memorable.

3. Abbey of Saint-Amand-de-Coly
Address: Le Bourg, 24290 Saint-Amand-de-Coly, France.

Tucked away in the village of Saint-Amand-de-Coly, this abbey is considered one of the most beautiful in Périgord. The fortified church, with its robust walls and narrow windows, reflects its turbulent history. As I explored the abbey, the contrast between its austere exterior and the peaceful interior was striking. The simplicity and elegance of the architecture, along with the quietude of the surrounding village, made this visit a deeply reflective experience.

4. Church of Saint-Léon-sur-Vézère

Address:Le Bourg, 24290 Saint-Léon-sur-Vézère, France.

Perched above the Vézère River, the Church of Saint-Léon-sur-Vézère is a charming Romanesque church dating back to the 12th century. The church's location, surrounded by lush greenery and overlooking the river, adds to its serene beauty. Inside, the simplicity of the stone construction and the light filtering through the small windows create a tranquil atmosphere perfect for contemplation.

5. Abbey of Brantôme
Address: 2 Rue Puyjoli de Meyjounissas, 24310 Brantôme en Périgord, France.

Known as the "Venice of Périgord," Brantôme is home to a beautiful Benedictine abbey built into the cliffs. The abbey's bell tower, one of the oldest in France, is a standout feature. Exploring the abbey, I was fascinated by the troglodyte caves that were used by monks and the picturesque gardens that invite quiet strolls. The sound of the Dronne River flowing nearby added to the peaceful ambiance of the site.
Tips
- Guided Tours: Many abbeys and churches offer guided tours, which are highly recommended to gain a deeper understanding of their historical and cultural significance.

- Timing Your Visit: Visiting early in the morning or later in the afternoon can provide a more serene experience, allowing you to appreciate the beauty and tranquility of these sacred spaces without the crowds.

- Combine Visits: Plan your route to visit multiple sites in one day. For instance, you can explore the Abbey of Brantôme in the morning and then head to Saint-Front Cathedral in Périgueux for the afternoon.

Exploring the abbeys and churches of Dordogne is like stepping back in time. Each site offers a unique glimpse into the region's spiritual heritage, architectural brilliance, and the quiet, enduring faith of its people. These sacred places are not just historical monuments; they are living parts of the communities that cherish and maintain them. As you wander through these holy sites, let the sense of history and serenity envelop you, enriching your journey through this beautiful region.

CHAPTER 5.

OUTDOOR ACTIVITIES AND NATURE

In the heart of the Dordogne region lies a playground for outdoor enthusiasts and nature lovers alike. This chapter invites you to explore the breathtaking landscapes, verdant forests, and meandering rivers that make Dordogne a haven for outdoor adventure. From leisurely strolls along scenic trails to adrenaline-pumping activities like kayaking and rock climbing, there's something for everyone to enjoy amidst the natural beauty of Dordogne. So lace up your hiking boots, grab your binoculars, and get ready to immerse yourself in the great outdoors of this captivating region.

Hiking and Walking Trails

Dordogne is a paradise for hikers and walkers, offering a myriad of trails that wind through picturesque countryside, ancient forests, and charming villages. Whether you're seeking a leisurely stroll or a challenging trek, the region's diverse landscapes promise unforgettable outdoor adventures.

How to get there
Many hiking and walking trails in Dordogne are easily accessible by car, with trailheads located near towns and villages throughout the region. Some trails may require a short drive from your accommodation, so be sure to plan your route in advance and check for parking options.

Addresses and Trailhead Locations

1. La Roque-Gageac to Domme Trail
Address: La Roque-Gageac, 24250, France.

- This scenic trail begins in the picturesque village of La Roque-Gageac and winds its way along the Dordogne River to the medieval town of Domme. The trail offers stunning views of the river and surrounding countryside, with plenty of opportunities to explore charming villages and historic sites along the way.

As I embarked on the La Roque-Gageac to Domme Trail, the tranquility of the countryside enveloped me, and the gentle rustle of leaves in the breeze provided a soothing soundtrack to my hike. The trail meandered through rolling hills and lush vineyards, with each turn revealing a new vista of the majestic Dordogne River below. Along the way, I encountered quaint stone bridges, centuries-old chapels, and rustic farmhouses, each adding to the charm and character of the landscape.

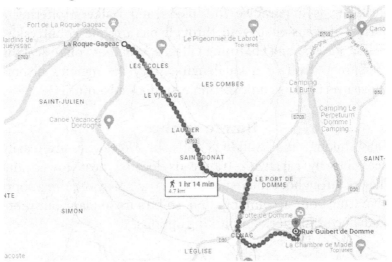

Explore scenic countryside, ancient forests, and charming villages along the trails. Enjoy breathtaking views of rivers, valleys, and limestone cliffs. Discover hidden caves, grottos, and prehistoric sites. Take leisurely breaks for picnics, wildlife spotting, and relaxation amidst nature

2. Circuit des Falaises
Address: Les Eyzies-de-Tayac-Sireuil, 24620, France.
   - This circular trail starts in the village of Les Eyzies-de-Tayac-Sireuil and takes hikers on a journey through the stunning Vézère Valley. The trail passes by dramatic limestone cliffs, prehistoric caves, and lush forests, offering a glimpse into the region's rich history and natural beauty.

The Circuit des Falaises offered a more rugged and adventurous experience, as I navigated narrow paths that hugged the edge of towering limestone cliffs. The sheer magnitude of the cliffs was awe-inspiring, and I couldn't help but marvel at the forces of nature that had sculpted such dramatic formations over millions of years. As I explored hidden caves and grottos tucked away along the trail, I felt a sense of wonder and reverence for the ancient landscapes of Dordogne.

3.Boucle des Pêcheurs
 - Address: Limeuil, 24510, France.
 - Starting in the charming village of Limeuil, this loop trail follows the banks of the Dordogne and Vézère rivers, offering breathtaking views of the surrounding countryside. Along the way, hikers can enjoy peaceful riverside picnics, explore hidden beaches, and discover ancient ruins.

In Limeuil, the Boucle des Pêcheurs provided a peaceful retreat along the tranquil banks of the Dordogne and Vézère rivers. The sound of rushing water and the gentle chirping of birds filled the air as I wandered through shaded forests and sun-dappled meadows. I paused to admire the reflections of medieval stone houses in the crystal-clear waters of the rivers, feeling a deep sense of connection to the timeless beauty of the natural world.

Recommendations
-Pack Essentials: Be sure to bring plenty of water, sunscreen, insect repellent, and sturdy footwear.
- Check Trail Conditions: Before setting out, check trail conditions and weather forecasts to ensure a safe and enjoyable hike.
- Respect Nature: Leave no trace, and respect wildlife and natural habitats along the trails.
- Take Your Time: Don't rush; take the time to pause, appreciate the scenery, and soak in the tranquility of the natural surroundings.

Hiking and walking in Dordogne offer a truly immersive way to experience the region's stunning landscapes and rich cultural heritage. Whether you're exploring ancient forests, meandering along riverside paths, or wandering through charming villages, each step reveals a new adventure waiting to be discovered. So lace up your hiking boots, hit the trails, and let the beauty of Dordogne inspire your next outdoor escape.

Canoeing and Kayaking on the Dordogne River

Immerse yourself in the natural beauty of Dordogne with an unforgettable canoeing or kayaking adventure on the picturesque Dordogne River. Paddling along its tranquil waters offers a unique perspective of the region's stunning landscapes, medieval castles, and charming riverside villages. Whether you're a novice or an experienced paddler, exploring the Dordogne by canoe or kayak promises an exhilarating outdoor experience.

How to get there

The Dordogne River is easily accessible from various points throughout the region. Canoe and kayak rental companies are scattered along the riverbanks in towns such as La Roque-Gageac, Beynac-et-Cazenac, and Vitrac. Most rental companies offer shuttle services to transport you to the starting point of your paddling adventure.

As you glide along the tranquil waters of the Dordogne River, you'll be treated to breathtaking views of towering limestone cliffs, lush greenery, and centuries-old castles perched atop rocky outcrops. Take your time to paddle at a leisurely pace, allowing yourself to fully appreciate the natural beauty that surrounds you.

Stop off at riverside beaches for a picnic lunch or a refreshing swim in the cool waters of the Dordogne. Explore hidden caves and alcoves along the riverbanks, where you can marvel at ancient rock formations and perhaps even spot some local wildlife, such as kingfishers or herons.

For a truly memorable experience, consider embarking on a multi-day paddling expedition along the Dordogne River. Camping along the riverbanks under the starry night sky adds an extra element of adventure to your journey, allowing you to connect with nature in a profound and meaningful way.

Rental Locations
- Kayak Adventures: Beynac-et-Cazenac, 24220, France.

- Dordogne River Explorers: Vitrac, 24200, France.

Recommendations

- Wear sunscreen and a hat to protect yourself from the sun.
- Bring plenty of water and snacks to stay hydrated and energized.
- Pack a waterproof bag to keep your belongings dry.
- Follow safety guidelines provided by the rental company, and always wear a life jacket while on the water.

Canoeing and kayaking on the Dordogne River offer a thrilling opportunity to explore the natural wonders of Dordogne at your own pace. Whether you're seeking a leisurely paddle or an adventurous expedition, the tranquil waters and scenic landscapes of the Dordogne River promise an unforgettable outdoor adventure. So grab a paddle, embark on a river journey, and let the beauty of Dordogne captivate your senses.

Cycling Routes and Rentals

Explore the breathtaking landscapes and charming villages of Dordogne on two wheels with an exhilarating cycling adventure. Whether you're a seasoned cyclist or a leisurely rider, the region offers a variety of cycling routes to suit every skill level. Pedal your way through rolling vineyards, ancient forests, and scenic countryside, and discover the beauty of Dordogne at your own pace.

How to get there

Dordogne boasts numerous bike rental shops and cycling routes accessible from towns and villages across the region. Depending on your starting point and preferred route, you can easily access cycling trails by car or public transportation. Rental shops often provide maps and recommendations for the best cycling routes based on your interests and experience level.

During your visit to dordogne, embark on a cycling journey through the picturesque landscapes, where each turn of the pedal reveals a new and breathtaking vista. Explore charming villages, medieval castles, and historic landmarks along well-marked cycling routes that cater to riders of all abilities.

Discover the region's rich cultural heritage as you cycle past ancient churches, traditional farmhouses, and rustic windmills nestled amidst rolling hills and sun-dappled vineyards. Take leisurely breaks to sample local delicacies at roadside cafes and farmer's markets, where you can indulge in freshly baked pastries, artisan cheeses, and gourmet chocolates.

For a more adventurous experience, venture off the beaten path and explore rugged mountain trails, dense forests, and hidden valleys that offer a glimpse into the untamed beauty of Dordogne's natural landscape. Keep an eye out for wildlife such as deer, wild boar, and rare bird species that call this region home.

Rental Locations

- Pedal Power: Sarlat-la-Canéda, 24200, France.

-Wheels of Dordogne: Bergerac, 24100, France.

- Cycle Adventures: Périgueux, 24000, France.

Tips

- Rent a bike that suits your height and riding style, and ensure it is properly fitted before setting off.
- Wear comfortable clothing and sturdy footwear suitable for cycling, and don't forget to bring a helmet for safety.
- Pack a picnic lunch and plenty of water to stay hydrated during your ride.
- Take breaks to rest and admire the scenery, and don't hesitate to ask locals for recommendations or assistance if needed.

Cycling in Dordogne offers a unique opportunity to immerse yourself in the region's natural beauty and cultural heritage while enjoying the freedom and flexibility of exploring at your own pace. Whether you're pedaling along scenic country lanes, traversing rugged mountain trails, or meandering through historic villages, the cycling routes of Dordogne promise unforgettable experiences and breathtaking vistas around every corner. So hop on your bike, embrace the open road, and let the adventure begin!

Wildlife Watching and Nature Reserves

Exploring the wildlife and nature reserves of Dordogne is a must for any nature enthusiast. This region is home to a diverse array of flora and fauna, and its well-preserved natural habitats provide a sanctuary for various species. Here's a detailed look at the best spots for wildlife watching and how to make the most of your time there.

Dordogne's nature reserves and wildlife-watching spots are easily accessible by car, with many located within a short drive from major towns and villages. Some reserves may also be reachable by public transportation or organized tours, depending on their location and accessibility.

1. Réserve Naturelle des Marais de Groléjac
- Address: 24250 Groléjac, France
How to get there: The reserve is located about 20 minutes from Sarlat-la-Canéda, accessible via the D46 road.

Réserve Naturelle des Marais de Groléjac is a wetland reserve that offers a unique ecosystem teeming with life. The area is a haven for birdwatchers, with species such as herons, kingfishers, and various waterfowl making their home here. Walking trails and observation points are scattered throughout the reserve, allowing you to immerse yourself in the natural surroundings and catch glimpses of the wildlife.

One morning, I found myself quietly sitting at one of the observation points, binoculars in hand. The early morning mist was just lifting, and I spotted a family of ducks gliding across the water, while a heron stood majestically on the shore. It was a serene experience, feeling connected to nature in such a peaceful setting.

2. Réserve Naturelle de la Vallée de l'Homme
Address: 24620 Les Eyzies, France
How to get there: The reserve is located near Les Eyzies, about a 30-minute drive from Périgueux via the D710 and D47 roads.

This reserve, also known as the Valley of Man, not only offers stunning landscapes but is also rich in prehistoric sites. As you hike through the trails, you'll encounter limestone cliffs, dense forests, and the Vezere River, all contributing to a biodiverse environment. Look out for deer, wild boar, and a variety of bird species as you explore the trails. The reserve also features educational panels that provide information about the local wildlife and the area's prehistoric significance.

During my visit, I hiked a trail that led me through a dense forest. The sounds of birds singing and leaves rustling in the wind created a symphony of nature. At one point, I was lucky enough to see a deer grazing in a clearing. It was a magical moment that underscored the untouched beauty of the reserve.

3. Réserve Zoologique de Calviac
Address: 24370 Calviac-en-Périgord, France
How to get there: Located about 15 minutes from Sarlat-la-Canéda, accessible via the D703 road.

Réserve Zoologique de Calviac is a wildlife reserve dedicated to the conservation of endangered species. This reserve features various habitats that are home to animals from around the world, including lemurs, wallabies, and maned wolves. The park is designed to educate visitors about wildlife conservation while providing an enjoyable experience. Walking paths wind through the different enclosures, offering close-up views of the animals in settings that mimic their natural habitats.

I spent an entire afternoon here, wandering from one exhibit to another. Watching the lemurs play and seeing the majestic maned wolves up close were highlights of my visit. The park's focus on conservation added an educational element that made the experience even more meaningful.

4. Parc Naturel Régional Périgord Limousin
- Address: 24360 Busserolles, France
- How to get there: The park is accessible from various points in Dordogne, with the main entrance near Busserolles, about an hour's drive from Périgueux via the N21 and D15 roads.

This regional natural park spans a vast area, offering a diverse range of landscapes, from rolling hills and dense forests to rivers and wetlands. The park is a sanctuary for wildlife, including otters, deer, and numerous bird species. There are numerous trails and guided tours available, catering to all levels of hikers. You can also engage in activities like fishing, horseback riding, and cycling.

Tips

- Bring Binoculars: To enhance your wildlife watching experience, bring a pair of binoculars. They will help you spot animals from a distance without disturbing them.
- Wear Appropriate Clothing: Dress in layers and wear sturdy walking shoes. Early mornings and late afternoons can be cool, while midday might be warmer.
- Be Patient and Quiet: Wildlife can be elusive. Patience and silence are key to observing animals in their natural habitats.
- Pack a Picnic: Many reserves have designated picnic areas. Packing a lunch allows you to spend more time enjoying the natural beauty.
- Respect the Environment: Follow the reserve's rules and guidelines. Stay on designated paths, do not disturb the wildlife, and take your trash with you.

Exploring the wildlife and nature reserves of Dordogne offers a perfect blend of adventure and tranquility. Each reserve provides a unique glimpse into the region's rich biodiversity, making it an ideal destination for nature lovers and wildlife enthusiasts. Whether you're an avid birdwatcher, a hiker, or someone who simply enjoys being in nature, Dordogne's natural wonders will leave you with unforgettable memories and a deeper appreciation for the environment.

Gardens and Parks

The gardens and parks of Dordogne offer serene sanctuaries where you can relax, explore, and connect with nature. With a variety of beautifully landscaped gardens and lush parks, there's no shortage of places to immerse yourself in the region's natural beauty.

1. Les Jardins de Marqueyssac
Address: 24220 Vézac, France
Located near the village of Vézac, Les Jardins de Marqueyssac is easily accessible by car. From Sarlat-la-Canéda, it's just a 15-minute drive via the D57 road.

Les Jardins de Marqueyssac is a stunning example of French formal gardens, with winding paths, clipped boxwood hedges, and breathtaking views over the Dordogne Valley. As you wander through the labyrinth of greenery, you'll find yourself enchanted by the intricate designs and the calming ambiance of the garden. Be sure to visit the Belvedere viewpoint for a panoramic vista of the valley and the meandering Dordogne River below.

One summer afternoon, I strolled through these gardens, the scent of lavender and rosemary in the air. I found a secluded bench under a shaded pergola and sat there, soaking in the tranquility and the stunning views. It was a perfect moment of peace and reflection.

2. Les Jardins d'Eyrignac
Address:24590 Salignac-Eyvigues, France

Les Jardins d'Eyrignac is located about 20 minutes by car from Sarlat-la-Canéda, accessible via the D6 and D60 roads. It boasts an impressive collection of topiary art, water features, and meticulously maintained flower beds. The gardens offer a unique blend of classical French and Italian styles, with each section presenting a different theme and mood. Take a leisurely walk through the White Garden, admire the rose garden in full bloom, and enjoy the serenity of the water garden.

When I visited Les Jardins d'Eyrignac, I was struck by the sheer artistry of the topiaries. The garden felt like a living sculpture gallery, each plant meticulously shaped into whimsical forms. It was a magical experience, wandering through this living artwork.

3. Jardins Panoramiques de Limeuil
Address: Place des Fossés, 24510 Limeuil, France
Situated in the village of Limeuil, these gardens are about a 30-minute drive from Bergerac, accessible via the D703 and D660 roads.

Perched on a hilltop at the confluence of the Dordogne and Vézère rivers, Jardins Panoramiques de Limeuil offers not only beautifully landscaped gardens but also sweeping views of the surrounding countryside. The gardens are divided into thematic sections, including a medicinal plant garden, a water garden, and a rose garden. It's an ideal spot for a picnic, with several scenic viewpoints and shaded areas to relax.

4. Parc le Bournat

Address: Allée Paul-Jean Souriau, 24260 Le Bugue, France

Parc le Bournat is located in Le Bugue, about a 40-minute drive from Périgueux, accessible via the D710 road. It's a unique park that combines the beauty of nature with a glimpse into traditional rural life in the 19th century. This living museum features beautifully landscaped gardens, historical buildings, and interactive exhibits. Wander through the vegetable gardens, admire the vibrant flower beds, and learn about traditional farming and crafts. There are also opportunities for hands-on activities, such as bread-making and pottery.

My visit to Parc le Bournat was like stepping back in time. I watched a blacksmith at work and even tried my hand at weaving. The combination of lush gardens and historical exhibits provided a rich and immersive experience.

Tips for Visiting Gardens and Parks in Dordogne

- Plan Your Visit: Check the opening hours and any special events or tours that might be available. Many gardens offer guided tours that provide deeper insights into the history and design.

- Wear Comfortable Shoes:*Gardens and parks can cover large areas, so be prepared for a lot of walking.

- Bring a Picnic: Many gardens and parks have designated picnic areas. Bringing your own food allows you to enjoy a leisurely meal surrounded by nature.

- Take Your Time: Gardens are meant to be savored slowly. Take time to sit and absorb the beauty around you, whether it's on a bench, under a tree, or beside a fountain.
- Photography: These locations are perfect for photography, so don't forget your camera. Capture the stunning landscapes and the intricate details of the flora.

Exploring the gardens and parks of Dordogne offers a perfect blend of relaxation and discovery. Each garden has its own unique charm and beauty, providing a peaceful retreat from the hustle and bustle of everyday life. Whether you're an avid gardener, a nature lover, or simply looking for a tranquil place to unwind, Dordogne's gardens and parks will leave you with lasting memories and a deep appreciation for the natural beauty of the region.

Hidden Gems and Off-the-Beaten-Path Destinations

Discovering hidden gems and off-the-beaten-path destinations in Dordogne is like uncovering buried treasures, each one offering its own unique charm and allure. While the region is known for its popular attractions and iconic landmarks, there are countless hidden gems waiting to be explored by adventurous travelers seeking something beyond the ordinary.

For those seeking a taste of rural charm, the village of Saint-Jean-de-Côle is a hidden gem worth discovering. This picturesque village, nestled in the heart of the Périgord Vert region, is known for its flower-filled streets, historic buildings, and tranquil riverside setting. Visit the beautifully restored Château de la Marthonie, stroll through the scenic Jardin des Moines, and immerse yourself in the laid-back atmosphere of this idyllic French village.

Another off-the-beaten-path destination worth exploring is the village of Limeuil, situated at the confluence of the Dordogne and Vézère rivers. This charming village is designated as one of the "Plus Beaux Villages de France" (Most Beautiful Villages of France) and is renowned for its scenic beauty and rich history. Explore the winding streets lined with half-timbered houses, visit the picturesque riverside gardens, and take a leisurely boat ride along the tranquil waters of the Dordogne River.

In addition to these hidden gems, Dordogne is home to countless other off-the-beaten-path destinations waiting to be discovered. Whether you're exploring secluded hiking trails, stumbling upon ancient ruins, or uncovering hidden waterfalls, each discovery adds to the magic and allure of this enchanting region. So venture off the beaten path, and you'll be rewarded with unforgettable experiences and memories that will last a lifetime.

CHAPTER 6.

EXPERIENCING DORDOGNE

Experiencing Dordogne is about immersing yourself in the heart and soul of this enchanting region. It's not just about visiting its stunning sites but about feeling the pulse of its everyday life. From savoring local delicacies at bustling markets to participating in traditional festivals, each moment spent in Dordogne is a step closer to understanding its rich cultural tapestry.

Must try dishes and Local Specialties

As a food enthusiast exploring the culinary delights of Dordogne, I couldn't wait to dive into the local specialties and dishes that define the region's gastronomic identity. From savory classics to sweet indulgences, each dish promised a journey of flavors and a glimpse into the rich culinary heritage of Dordogne.

Here are some must-try dishes that will take your taste buds on a journey through the heart of Dordogne:

1. Foie Gras: My first encounter with foie gras was a revelation. Served in a terrine with crusty bread and sweet fig jam, the creamy richness of the foie gras melted on my tongue, leaving behind a lingering sweetness and a hint of earthy flavor. It was a decadent indulgence that I savored with every bite, savoring the contrast of textures and the complexity of flavors. For those with dietary restrictions or ethical concerns, consider

exploring alternative options or substitutes, such as plant-based foie gras or pâtés made from sustainable sources.

2. Truffles: Truffle season in Dordogne is a culinary event not to be missed, and my first taste of this prized delicacy was nothing short of extraordinary. Shaved over a simple pasta dish, the intoxicating aroma of black truffles filled the air, transporting me to a realm of culinary bliss. Each bite was a symphony of earthy flavors and delicate nuances, a testament to the truffle's status as the "black diamond" of the culinary world. For those with allergies or sensitivities to truffles, be sure to inquire about ingredient substitutions or opt for truffle-free dishes.

3. Magret de Canard: A quintessential dish of Dordogne, magret de canard is a celebration of the region's prized duck meat. Grilled to perfection and served with a tangy berry sauce, my first taste of magret de canard was a revelation. The tender meat, with its rich flavor and crispy skin, paired perfectly with the sweet and tart notes of the sauce, creating a harmonious balance of flavors. For those with dietary restrictions, consider exploring alternative protein options or opting for leaner cuts of duck meat.

4. Walnut Cake: Dordogne's walnut cake is a beloved dessert that captures the essence of the region's bounty. My first bite of this delectable treat was pure bliss – the moist and nutty cake, studded with crunchy walnuts and drizzled with honey, was a symphony of flavors and textures. It was the perfect ending to a meal, a sweet reminder of Dordogne's culinary prowess. For those with nut allergies, be sure to inquire about alternative dessert options or consider homemade walnut-free versions.

5. Cabécou: This small goat cheese, native to Dordogne, stole my heart with its creamy texture and tangy flavor. Served alongside crusty bread and local honey, my first taste of cabécou was a revelation. The rich and buttery cheese, with its subtle earthiness and hints of sweetness, paired perfectly with the sweet and floral notes of the honey, creating a harmonious balance of flavors. For those with lactose intolerance or dairy allergies, consider exploring alternative cheese options made from non-dairy sources or opting for lactose-free varieties.

6. Duck Confit: Tender and succulent, duck confit is a cornerstone of Périgord cuisine. The duck is slowly cooked in its own fat until it's melt-in-your-mouth tender, then crisped to perfection. Served with golden potatoes and a side of tangy greens, this dish is a true taste of the Dordogne.

7. Crème Brûlée: While not exclusive to Dordogne, crème brûlée takes on a special significance when enjoyed amidst the region's picturesque scenery. Delight in the creamy custard topped with a layer of caramelized sugar, creating a contrast of textures and flavors that will leave you craving more. The soft glow of the candle lit up the dessert menu, making every word seem like a delicious promise. But my attention was drawn to one particular item: "Crème Brûlée Maison." Maison – homemade. Here, in a cozy bistro tucked away on a quaint street in Sarlat-la-Canéda, this crème brûlée wasn't just any dessert; it was a local legend.

As you embark on your culinary journey through Dordogne, remember to savor each bite and embrace the flavors of the region with an open mind and adventurous spirit. Be sure to communicate any dietary restrictions or allergies to your server, and don't hesitate to ask for ingredient substitutions or modifications to accommodate your needs. With its rich culinary heritage and diverse array of dishes, Dordogne offers something for every palate and dietary preference, ensuring a memorable dining experience for all.

Wine Regions and Vineyard Tours

Dordogne's wine regions are a paradise for oenophiles and casual wine enthusiasts alike. The region's rolling hills and fertile valleys produce some of France's most exquisite wines. Exploring these vineyards offers a blend of scenic beauty, rich history, and, of course, delicious wines.

The most renowned wine area in Dordogne is Bergerac, home to numerous esteemed vineyards. To start your wine journey, head to the charming town of Bergerac itself. From there, you can easily access many vineyards by car or even by bike if you're up for a scenic ride through the countryside. The Maison des Vins de Bergerac, located at Quai Cyrano, 1 rue des Récollets, 24100 Bergerac, is a great place to begin. Here, you can learn about the local wines and pick up a map of nearby vineyards.

A visit to Château de Monbazillac (Address: Monbazillac, 24240, France) is a must. This historic vineyard not only offers tastings of their famous sweet wines but also a tour of the picturesque château and its gardens. To get there, drive south from Bergerac on the D936 road and follow the signs for Monbazillac

One memorable visit was to Château de Tiregand (Address: Pécharmant, 24100, France). This family-run estate in the Pécharmant appellation is known for its robust red wines. The owner's passion was evident during the tour, as they explained the winemaking process and shared stories of their family's winemaking heritage. The vineyard is just a short drive from Bergerac, accessible via the D21 road.

For a more intimate experience, I recommend visiting smaller, lesser-known vineyards like Domaine de l'Ancienne Cure (Address: 1 Chemin de Tirecul, 24240 Colombier, France). This vineyard, nestled in the rolling hills near Colombier, offers personalized tours and tastings. The winemaker, Christian Roche, took us through his vineyards, explaining the organic methods he uses to produce his wines. It was fascinating to see the care and dedication that goes into each bottle. To visit, drive along the D13 from Bergerac towards Sigoulès.

To make the most of your vineyard tours, try to visit during the harvest season in late summer or early autumn. This is when the vineyards are bustling with activity, and you might even get the chance to see the grape harvesting process in action.

Don't forget to enjoy the local cuisine paired with the wines you're tasting. Many vineyards have on-site restaurants or picnic areas where you can enjoy a meal surrounded by the vines. The blend of Dordogne's culinary delights with its wines creates an unforgettable experience.

Each vineyard visit is not just about tasting wine but about connecting with the history and passion behind each bottle. Whether you're a seasoned wine connoisseur or just beginning to explore the world of wine, Dordogne's vineyards offer something special. So, raise a glass and toast to the enchanting wine regions of Dordogne!

Markets and Artisanal Products

Dordogne is a haven for food lovers, offering a rich tapestry of farmers markets and artisanal products that reflect the region's bountiful harvests and culinary traditions. Visiting these markets is an essential part of experiencing Dordogne, allowing you to immerse yourself in the local culture and taste the freshest produce.

Start your exploration with the famous market in Sarlat-la-Canéda. Held every Wednesday and Saturday morning in the Place de la Liberté, this market is a feast for the senses. The air is filled with the scent of fresh bread, ripe fruit, and fragrant herbs. Vendors proudly display their goods, from vibrant vegetables to handmade cheeses and charcuterie. The market is a short walk from the town center, making it easy to explore the medieval streets before or after your visit.

In the town of Bergerac, the twice-weekly market on Place Gambetta is a must-visit. Every Wednesday and Saturday morning, the square transforms into a bustling marketplace. Here, you can find an array of local specialties, such as foie gras, truffles, and walnuts. The atmosphere is lively, with locals chatting and bargaining with vendors. To get there, simply head to the town center.

For a more intimate experience, the market in Issigeac is perfect. This Sunday market, held in the heart of this picturesque medieval village, is renowned for its charm and variety. Stalls line the narrow streets, offering everything from fresh produce to artisanal crafts. As you wander, you might find yourself drawn to a stall selling handmade soaps or local honey. To visit, drive to Issigeac via the D25 from Bergerac.

One of my favorite experiences was at the market in Périgueux. This market offers a vibrant mix of food, flowers, and crafts. I remember tasting a slice of warm walnut cake from a vendor and being enchanted by the rich, nutty flavor. The market is located in the town center, making it easy to combine with a visit to Périgueux's historic sites.

In addition to the markets, Dordogne is famous for its artisanal products. One standout is the truffle, often referred to as "black gold." Many local producers offer truffle hunts, where you can join a trained dog in searching for these elusive delicacies. One such experience is offered by Truffière de Pechalifour (Address: Pechalifour, 24260 Saint-Cyprien, France).To get there, drive from Saint-Cyprien on the D703 road.

Another highlight is the walnut oil, a regional specialty. Visit the Moulin de la Veyssière (Address: 24190 Neuvic, France), an old mill where you can see the traditional process of making walnut oil and taste the delicious results. The mill is located on the banks of the Isle River, accessible via the D43 road from Neuvic.

To make the most of your market visits, arrive early to avoid the crowds and enjoy the freshest produce. Take the time to chat with the vendors; their passion for their products is contagious and they can offer valuable tips on how to best enjoy your purchases.

Exploring the markets and artisanal products of Dordogne is not just about shopping; it's about experiencing the region's way of life. The flavors, aromas, and interactions create memories that stay with you long after your visit. So, bring a basket, your curiosity, and a hearty appetite to discover the culinary treasures of Dordogne.

Festivals and Events

Dordogne is a region that celebrates its rich history, culture, and culinary heritage with a vibrant array of festivals and events throughout the year. These gatherings offer visitors a unique opportunity to immerse themselves in the local traditions and enjoy the lively atmosphere that defines the Dordogne experience.

One of the most anticipated events is the Sarlat Truffle Festival, held every January in Sarlat-la-Canéda. This festival is a truffle lover's dream, showcasing the prized black truffle of Périgord. The streets of Sarlat come alive with market stalls, cooking demonstrations, and truffle hunts. You can taste truffle-infused dishes, attend truffle auctions, and even participate in workshops. To get there, head to the town center of Sarlat.

Another must-visit is the Bergerac Wine Festival, celebrated every August. This event is a tribute to the region's wine heritage, featuring tastings, vineyard tours, and music. The festival takes place in various locations around Bergerac, with the main events happening in the town center. To get to Bergerac, take the D933 from Bordeaux or the D936 from Périgueux.

The "Félibrée Festival" is a traditional Occitan celebration that rotates among different villages in Dordogne each year, usually in July. This festival celebrates the Occitan culture with parades, folk music, dancing, and traditional costumes. It's a colorful, lively event where you can experience the local customs and enjoy regional food.

For a taste of medieval history, the Festival du Périgord Noir offers a series of concerts, often held in historic venues like castles and churches, from July to August. The music ranges from classical to contemporary, providing a magical experience in the heart of the Périgord Noir. Concerts are spread across various locations, including Sarlat, Périgueux, and other towns. Visit (www.festivalmusiqueperigordnoir.com) for the program and ticket information.

The La Félibrée** August is another highlight, especially in the town of Domme. This event showcases local crafts, music, and traditional dance. Streets are decorated, and the community comes together to celebrate their heritage. Domme can be reached via the D703 road from Sarlat.

One unforgettable experience was at the Marché des Producteurs de Pays (Local Producers' Market) in Périgueux. These markets occur in various towns during summer evenings and feature local farmers selling their produce. The market in Périgueux is held every Wednesday evening in July and August at Place Saint-Louis. It was a joy to mingle with locals, taste freshly prepared dishes, and enjoy live music under the stars. To get there, head to the town center.

For those interested in film, the Festival du Film de Sarlat is a notable event held every November. This festival screens a variety of French and international films, offering a chance to see new releases and attend discussions with filmmakers. It takes place in various venues around Sarlat-la-Canéda. Check the festival's schedule at (www.festivaldufilmdesarlat.com)

When attending these festivals, it's essential to arrive early to find good parking and secure a spot for the events. Each festival offers a unique glimpse into Dordogne's culture, so take the time to explore, interact with locals, and savor the regional specialties.

The festivals and events in Dordogne provide a vibrant and engaging way to experience the local culture. Whether you're tasting truffles, enjoying a glass of Bergerac wine, or dancing to Occitan music, each event offers memories that will last a lifetime. So, mark your calendar and get ready to join in the celebrations that make Dordogne truly special.

Recommended Restaurants and Cafés

The Dordogne Valley isn't just a feast for the eyes; it's a haven for the taste buds as well. From Michelin-starred artistry to cozy cafes brimming with local charm, there's something to tantalize every palate. Here are a few recommendations to get your Dordogne culinary adventure started, complete with addresses and travel tips:

Fine Dining:

Maison Lameloise (Périgueux): The crisp fall air made me shiver as I walked towards Maison Lameloise, a fancy restaurant in Périgueux. It had two Michelin stars, which meant it was really good but also really expensive.

Inside, the restaurant was fancy and quiet. The sunlight came in through big windows, making everything look shiny. The waiters wore nice clothes and moved around gracefully, like they were dancing.

When I sat down, I felt a little nervous. The menu was like a fancy book, with lots of delicious-sounding dishes. Each dish was like a work of art, made with fresh ingredients from the Dordogne region.

The first course was amazing, with lots of different flavors. Each bite was like a surprise. The next courses were just as good. The desserts were especially delicious, like a sweet symphony in my mouth.

After the meal, I felt happy and full. Even though it was expensive, the meal was worth it. It was like a special adventure for my taste buds.

But Maison Lameloise is just one part of the Dordogne story. This region has lots of other great places to eat, from fancy restaurants to cozy cafes. This travel guide will help you find them all.

This two-Michelin-starred haven of gastronomy is a must for serious foodies. Address: 2 Rue Fragneau, 24000 Périgueux, France. Getting There: Located in the heart of Périgueux, easily accessible by car or taxi. Public transportation options include a short walk from the Périgueux train station. Prepare to be pampered with an unforgettable culinary journey that showcases the best of Périgord cuisine, all crafted with seasonal ingredients and stunning presentation.

Casual Dining:
La Table de Martine (Montignac): Address: 5 Rue du Dr Roux, 24200 Montignac, France. Getting There: Situated just a short stroll from the famous Lascaux Caves, La Table de Martine is the perfect post-exploration pit stop. This cozy restaurant offers a warm and inviting atmosphere where you can savor delicious traditional fare. Think hearty stews, succulent roasts, and delectable desserts – all made with love and fresh, local ingredients.

Tip: For a truly local experience, ask about the daily specials, which often feature seasonal specialties.

Au Bistrot de Nath Sarlat-la-Canéda: Address: 5 Rue de la Petitevergne, 24200 Sarlat-la-Canéda, France. Getting There: Huddled in the heart of the charming town of Sarlat-la-Canéda, Au Bistrot de Nath is a haven for hearty appetites and friendly service. Prepare to be greeted with smiles and a menu brimming with Périgord classics. Don't miss their signature magret de canard duck breast, cooked to juicy perfection, and be sure to save room for their decadent chocolate mousse – a guaranteed Dordogne indulgence!

Cafes:
Café des Arts:
Address: 5 Place de la Myrpe, 24100 Bergerac, France. Getting There: Located in the historical center of Bergerac, Café des Arts is an ideal spot to relax, people-watch, and soak up the Dordogne atmosphere. Settle into a wicker chair on the terrace, sip on a cup of locally roasted coffee, or unwind with a glass of Bergerac wine. This charming cafe is the perfect place to observe the daily rhythms of Bergerac life.

Le Glacier des Marronniers (Sarlat-la-Canéda): Address: 30 Rue de la Salamandre, 24200 Sarlat-la-Canéda, France. (Getting There: A short walk from the main square in Sarlat-la-Canéda, Le Glacier des Marronniers is a haven for ice cream aficionados. This delightful parlor boasts a wide selection of homemade flavors, all crafted with fresh, local ingredients. From classic vanilla to decadent chocolate, and even adventurous options like lavender or walnut, there's a scoop to satisfy every craving. On a hot Dordogne afternoon, Le Glacier des Marronniers is a guaranteed recipe for cool refreshment.

Bonus Tip: Don't forget to explore the local markets! Many Dordogne villages and towns host weekly gatherings where you can find an abundance of fresh produce, local cheeses, artisan breads, and regional specialties. Imagine a picnic lunch spread with crusty baguettes, juicy tomatoes, creamy cheeses, and perhaps a slice of walnut cake – all enjoyed under the warm Dordogne sun. Alternatively, stock up on ingredients and create your own Dordogne feast in your vacation rental.

This is just a taste of the culinary delights that await you in the Dordogne Valley. From Michelin-starred artistry to hidden gems nestled in charming villages, the Dordogne's diverse culinary scene promises an unforgettable adventure for your taste buds. So, turn the page, and let's embark on this delicious journey together!

CHAPTER 7.

ITINERARIES

Dordogne 3-Day Getaway

Planning a three-day escape to Dordogne offers the perfect opportunity to immerse yourself in its historic charm, natural beauty, and delightful cuisine. Here's a detailed itinerary to help you make the most of your time in this captivating region.

Day 1: Discovering Sarlat-la-Canéda and Beynac-et-Cazenac

Morning: Sarlat-la-Canéda
Start your adventure in the picturesque town of Sarlat-la-Canéda. Wander through its medieval streets, marvel at the well-preserved Gothic and Renaissance architecture, and soak in the vibrant atmosphere. Don't miss the bustling Saturday market, where you can sample local produce, cheeses, and pastries. The town's central square, Place de la Liberté, is a great spot for people-watching and enjoying a café au lait.

Afternoon: Beynac-et-Cazenac
In the afternoon, take a short drive to Beynac-et-Cazenac, a stunning village perched on a cliff overlooking the Dordogne River. Visit the Château de Beynac, a fortress with breathtaking views of the valley. Explore the narrow, cobbled streets lined with honey-colored stone houses, and enjoy the serene ambiance.

Evening: Dinner in Sarlat-la-Canéda
Return to Sarlat-la-Canéda for dinner at one of its charming restaurants. Indulge in regional specialties like duck confit or foie gras, paired with a glass of local wine.

Day 2: Exploring the Prehistoric and Medieval Wonders

Morning: Lascaux Caves
Begin your second day with a visit to the Lascaux IV caves in Montignac. This modern replica of the original prehistoric cave art site offers an incredible glimpse into the lives of our ancient ancestors. The guided tour provides fascinating insights into the significance of these paintings.

Afternoon: La Roque-Gageac
Next, drive to La Roque-Gageac, a beautiful village nestled between a cliff and the Dordogne River. Take a leisurely boat trip on a traditional gabare to admire the scenic landscape and learn about the area's history. Afterward, explore the tropical gardens and winding lanes of the village.

Evening: Domme
In the evening, head to Domme, a seaside town offering panoramic views of the valley. Stroll through its medieval gates and explore the charming streets filled with artisan shops. Enjoy a meal at a local eatery, savoring dishes made with fresh, local ingredients.

Day 3: Embracing the Outdoors

Morning: Canoeing on the Dordogne River
Start your final day with a canoeing adventure on the Dordogne River. Rent a canoe from one of the local outfitters, such as Canoë Dordogne or Canoës Loisirs, and paddle through tranquil waters, passing by picturesque villages and lush countryside. It's a fantastic way to experience the natural beauty of the region.

Afternoon: Marqueyssac Gardens
After your canoeing excursion, visit the Gardens of Marqueyssac, renowned for their beautifully manicured boxwood hedges and panoramic views of the Dordogne Valley. Stroll through the winding paths, enjoy the shaded picnic spots, and be sure to visit the belvedere for breathtaking vistas.

Evening: Farewell Dinner in Sarlat-la-Canéda
Return to Sarlat-la-Canéda for a farewell dinner. Choose a cozy bistro and savor a final meal of regional specialties. Reflect on the wonderful experiences of the past three days and toast to the beauty and charm of Dordogne.

Getting Around
To fully enjoy this itinerary, renting a car is highly recommended. The flexibility allows you to explore at your own pace and visit all the must-see sites comfortably.

With this three-day getaway, you'll experience the best of Dordogne's history, culture, and natural beauty. From medieval towns and prehistoric caves to scenic river adventures and stunning gardens, this itinerary promises a memorable and enriching journey.

Dordogne One-Week Adventure

Embarking on a one-week adventure in Dordogne allows you to delve deeper into the region's rich history, breathtaking landscapes, and delightful cuisine. Here's a detailed itinerary to help you make the most of your time in this enchanting part of France.

Day 1: Arrival and Exploring Sarlat-la-Canéda

Morning: Arrival in Sarlat-la-Canéda
Begin your journey by arriving in the charming town of Sarlat-la-Canéda. Check into your accommodation and take a moment to settle in. The town offers a variety of options, from cozy bed and breakfasts to luxurious hotels.

Afternoon: Stroll Through Sarlat-la-Canéda
Spend the afternoon wandering through the medieval streets of Sarlat-la-Canéda. Marvel at the well-preserved Gothic and Renaissance architecture, visit the Cathedral of Saint-Sacerdos, and explore the lively market if it's a Wednesday or Saturday.

Evening: Dinner in Sarlat-la-Canéda
Enjoy dinner at one of the town's charming restaurants. Sample local delicacies like duck confit, foie gras, and walnut cake, paired with a glass of Bergerac wine.

Day 2: Beynac-et-Cazenac and La Roque-Gageac

Morning: Visit Beynac-et-Cazenac
Drive to the picturesque village of Beynac-et-Cazenac. Visit the impressive Château de Beynac, perched high on a cliff, offering stunning views of the Dordogne River and valley. Explore the narrow, cobbled streets and soak in the medieval atmosphere.

Afternoon: Explore La Roque-Gageac
Head to La Roque-Gageac, another beautiful village nestled along the Dordogne River. Take a leisurely boat trip on a traditional gabare to learn about the region's history and enjoy the scenic views.

Evening: Dinner with a View
Enjoy a riverside dinner in La Roque-Gageac. The village's restaurants offer a variety of local dishes and wines, with beautiful views of the river and surrounding cliffs.

Day 3: Prehistoric Wonders in Montignac
Morning: Lascaux IV Caves
Drive to Montignac to visit the Lascaux IV caves, a remarkable replica of the original prehistoric cave art site. Take a guided tour to learn about the significance of these ancient paintings and the lives of early humans.

Afternoon: Stroll Through Montignac

Explore the charming town of Montignac, with its medieval bridges, quaint streets, and riverside cafés. Have a leisurely lunch and enjoy the relaxed atmosphere.

Evening: Return to Sarlat-la-Canéda

Head back to Sarlat-la-Canéda for the night. If you have energy left, take an evening stroll through the town, which is beautifully lit up after dark.

Day 4: Castles and Gardens

Morning: Château de Castelnaud

Visit Château de Castelnaud, a medieval fortress with a fascinating history. Explore the museum of medieval warfare housed within the castle and enjoy the panoramic views from the ramparts.

Afternoon: Gardens of Marqueyssac

Head to the Gardens of Marqueyssac, famous for their beautifully manicured boxwood hedges and stunning views of the Dordogne Valley. Stroll through the winding paths and enjoy the peaceful surroundings.

Evening: Dinner in Domme

Drive to the bastide town of Domme for dinner. Enjoy a meal at a local restaurant and take in the panoramic views of the valley from the town's lookout points.

Day 5: Canoeing and Kayaking

Morning: Canoeing on the Dordogne River

Start your day with a canoeing adventure on the Dordogne River. Rent a canoe from one of the local outfitters, such as Canoë Dordogne or Canoës Loisirs, and paddle through tranquil waters, passing by picturesque villages and lush countryside.

Afternoon: Picnic by the River

Pack a picnic and stop along the riverbank to enjoy lunch surrounded by nature. Relax and soak in the peaceful atmosphere before continuing your canoe journey.

Evening: Return to Sarlat-la-Canéda

Head back to Sarlat-la-Canéda for the evening. Enjoy a relaxing dinner and reflect on your day's adventure.

Day 6: Exploring Périgueux

Morning: Drive to Périgueux

Set off for Périgueux, the capital of the Dordogne department. Visit the Saint-Front Cathedral, a stunning example of Byzantine architecture, and explore the Vesunna Gallo-Roman Museum, which showcases the region's ancient history.

Afternoon: Discover Périgueux

Wander through the old town, with its narrow streets, half-timbered houses, and lively markets. Enjoy a leisurely lunch at one of the city's many cafés and restaurants.

Evening: Return to Sarlat-la-Canéda

Make your way back to Sarlat-la-Canéda for the night. Enjoy a final dinner in town, savoring the local cuisine one last time.

Day 7: Final Day of Relaxation and Exploration
Morning: Market Day in Sarlat-la-Canéda
Spend your final morning exploring the market in Sarlat-la-Canéda. Pick up some local products to take home, such as truffle oil, walnut liqueur, and handmade crafts.

Afternoon: Relax and Reflect
Take some time to relax and reflect on your week in Dordogne. Visit any sites you may have missed or simply enjoy a peaceful afternoon in the town.

Evening: Farewell Dinner
Enjoy a farewell dinner at a restaurant in Sarlat-la-Canéda. Toast to a wonderful week filled with unforgettable experiences and memories.

Getting Around
To fully enjoy this itinerary, renting a car is highly recommended. The flexibility allows you to explore at your own pace and visit all the must-see sites comfortably. Public transportation is limited, and having a car makes it easier to access the region's many attractions.

With this one-week adventure, you'll experience the best of Dordogne's history, culture, and natural beauty. From medieval towns and prehistoric caves to scenic river adventures and stunning gardens, this itinerary promises a memorable and enriching journey.

Family-Friendly Itinerary

Planning a family-friendly trip to Dordogne ensures a mix of fun, adventure, and educational experiences for everyone. Here's a detailed itinerary to help you make the most of your family vacation in this beautiful region.

Day 1: Arrival and Exploring Sarlat-la-Canéda

Morning: Arrival in Sarlat-la-Canéda

Start your journey by arriving in Sarlat-la-Canéda, a town that feels like stepping into a fairy tale. Check into a family-friendly accommodation like Hôtel La Couleuvrine, which offers spacious rooms and a welcoming atmosphere.

Afternoon: Stroll Through Sarlat-la-Canéda

Spend the afternoon exploring the medieval streets of Sarlat-la-Canéda. The kids will love the narrow, winding alleys and the lively market (on Wednesdays and Saturdays). Stop for a treat at one of the local patisseries and let the kids pick out their favorite pastries.

Evening: Dinner in Sarlat-la-Canéda

Enjoy a family dinner at a local restaurant such as Le Presidial, which offers a children's menu and outdoor seating. Try the regional specialties while the kids enjoy simple yet delicious dishes.

Day 2: Adventure in Beynac-et-Cazenac

Morning: Visit Château de Beynac

Drive to Beynac-et-Cazenac and visit the impressive Château de Beynac. The castle's battlements and towers will fascinate the children, and the panoramic views are breathtaking.

Afternoon: Picnic and Explore Beynac
Pack a picnic and find a scenic spot along the river. After lunch, take a leisurely stroll through the village, exploring its charming streets and artisan shops.

Evening: Return to Sarlat-la-Canéda
Head back to Sarlat-la-Canéda for the evening. Relax at your hotel or take a twilight walk through the town.

Day 3: Fun in La Roque-Gageac

Morning: Boat Trip on the Dordogne River
Head to La Roque-Gageac for a boat trip on a traditional gabare. The kids will love the adventure, and you'll all learn about the region's history and enjoy the beautiful scenery.

Afternoon: Explore La Roque-Gageac
After your boat trip, explore La Roque-Gageac. Visit the tropical garden with its exotic plants, which is a hit with children, and enjoy a riverside lunch at a local café.

Evening: Dinner in La Roque-Gageac
Dine at one of the village's family-friendly restaurants. The outdoor seating and relaxed atmosphere are perfect for families.

Day 4: Prehistoric Adventure in Montignac
Morning: Lascaux IV Caves
Drive to Montignac to visit the Lascaux IV caves. The interactive exhibits and stunning cave paintings will captivate

both adults and children. The tour is designed to be engaging for kids, with a focus on discovery and adventure.

Afternoon: Stroll Through Montignac
Explore the town of Montignac, have lunch at a riverside café, and let the kids play in one of the local parks.

Evening: Return to Sarlat-la-Canéda
Return to your base in Sarlat-la-Canéda. Enjoy a relaxing evening with the family.

Day 5: Canoeing and Outdoor Fun

Morning: Canoeing on the Dordogne River
Rent canoes from Canoë Dordogne or Canoës Loisirs in La Roque-Gageac and set off for a family adventure on the river. The calm waters and stunning views make it a perfect activity for all ages.

Afternoon: Picnic and Swim
Find a suitable spot along the riverbank for a picnic and swimming. The kids will love splashing in the water, and you'll appreciate the serene surroundings.

Evening: Return to Sarlat-la-Canéda
Head back to Sarlat-la-Canéda. Enjoy dinner at a casual family-friendly restaurant, such as L'Adresse, which offers a range of dishes to suit all tastes.

Day 6: Gardens and Playtime

Morning: Gardens of Marqueyssac
Visit the Gardens of Marqueyssac, where the whole family can enjoy wandering through the beautifully manicured boxwood hedges. There are activities and trails designed for children, including a play area and educational exhibits.

Afternoon: Picnic and Explore
Have a picnic in the gardens, then explore more of the trails and play areas. The kids will love the adventure paths and discovering the hidden corners of the garden.

Evening: Return to Sarlat-la-Canéda
Return to Sarlat-la-Canéda for a relaxed evening. Maybe treat the family to ice cream from one of the town's gelaterias.

Day 7: Périgueux and Farewell

Morning: Drive to Périgueux
Drive to Périgueux for a final day of exploration. Visit the Vesunna Gallo-Roman Museum, where the interactive exhibits will keep the kids entertained while learning about ancient history.

Afternoon: Discover Périgueux
Wander through the old town, visit the Saint-Front Cathedral, and have lunch at a family-friendly café. Let the kids burn off some energy in a local park.

Evening: Return to Sarlat-la-CanédaHead back to Sarlat-la-Canéda for your final night. Have a farewell dinner at your favorite restaurant from the trip and reminisce about all the fun experiences.

Getting Around
For this family-friendly itinerary, renting a car is also essential. It allows you the flexibility to move at your own pace and ensures that all destinations are easily accessible. Public transportation options are limited, and having a car makes the trip much more convenient and enjoyable for the whole family.

With this carefully planned itinerary, your family will experience the best of Dordogne's history, nature, and culinary delights, creating lasting memories of your time in this enchanting region.

CHAPTER 8.

PRACTICAL TIPS AND ADVICE

Embarking on an adventure in Dordogne is thrilling, but having essential practical information ensures your trip goes smoothly. This chapter is designed to equip you with crucial details and tips to navigate the region confidently and enjoyably. From health and safety advice to communication tips, and from currency exchange to emergency contacts, we've got you covered. We'll also provide you with useful websites, apps, and maps to enhance your travel experience and help you make the most of your time in Dordogne. Get ready to explore with peace of mind, knowing you have all the practical insights at your fingertips.

Language and Communication

In the heart of the Dordogne region, where the valleys are lush and the villages picturesque, language and communication take on a delightful charm of their own. While French is the predominant language spoken here, you'll find that the locals are often welcoming and accommodating to those who make an effort to communicate, regardless of linguistic proficiency.

French is the official language of France, and learning a few key phrases can go a long way in enhancing your experience in the Dordogne. Simple greetings like "Bonjour" (hello) and "Merci" (thank you) are always appreciated and can help break the ice in any interaction. If you're feeling a bit adventurous, try practicing phrases like "Parlez-vous anglais?" (Do you speak English?) or "Pouvez-vous m'aider?" (Can you help me?), which can be useful when seeking assistance or information.

Engaging with locals in their native tongue can open doors to authentic experiences and cultural exchanges. Don't be afraid to stumble over your words; the effort alone is often met with warmth and encouragement. Many residents are proud of their language and heritage and appreciate visitors who show an interest in both.

In addition to spoken communication, non-verbal cues and body language play a significant role in conveying messages. A friendly smile, a nod of the head, or a gesture of appreciation can bridge any language barrier and foster meaningful connections with the people you encounter.

For those seeking additional language support, language translation apps and pocket phrase books can be valuable tools for navigating conversations and understanding local customs. However, don't rely solely on technology; sometimes, the best communication happens when you put down your device and engage with people face-to-face.

Ultimately, language and communication in the Dordogne are about more than just words; they're about connection and shared experiences. Embrace the opportunity to immerse yourself in the local language and culture, and you'll find that the bonds you form with the people you meet will enrich your travel experience in ways you never imagined.

Currency and Banking

Navigating currency and banking in Dordogne is essential for a hassle-free trip. The official currency in France is the Euro (€). Before you set out on your adventure, it's wise to familiarize yourself with a few key points about handling money in Dordogne.

1. Getting Euros Before Your Trip
Before you leave, consider exchanging some money into Euros at your local bank. Having a small amount of local currency on hand when you arrive can be convenient for immediate expenses like transportation, snacks, or tips. This saves you from the immediate need to find an ATM or currency exchange upon arrival.

2. Using ATMs
ATMs (known as "distributeurs de billets" in French) are widely available throughout Dordogne, especially in larger towns like Sarlat-la-Canéda, Périgueux, and Bergerac. They are usually the most cost-effective way to obtain Euros. Most ATMs accept major credit and debit cards, including Visa and MasterCard. When using an ATM, opt to be charged in Euros to avoid additional conversion fees.

3. Banking Hours and Locations

Banks in Dordogne generally operate from 9:00 AM to 5:00 PM, Monday to Friday, with a break for lunch around noon. Some banks may also open on Saturday mornings. It's helpful to locate the nearest bank branches in the towns you plan to visit. For instance, Crédit Agricole, BNP Paribas, and Société Générale have multiple branches across the region.

4. Credit and Debit Card Usage

Credit and debit cards are widely accepted in Dordogne, especially in hotels, restaurants, and larger shops. However, in smaller villages and local markets, cash is often preferred. Always carry some cash for such occasions. It's also a good idea to inform your bank of your travel plans to avoid any issues with card usage abroad.

5. Currency Exchange Services

Currency exchange services are available at airports, major train stations, and some hotels. However, they often charge higher fees and offer less favorable exchange rates than ATMs. If you need to exchange money, compare rates and fees to ensure you get the best deal.

6. Traveler's Cheques

Traveler's cheques are not commonly used or widely accepted in France, including Dordogne. It's better to rely on cards and cash for your transactions.

7. Tipping

In Dordogne, tipping is appreciated but not mandatory. A service charge is often included in restaurant bills, but if you receive excellent service, rounding up the bill or leaving a small tip (5-10%) is a nice gesture. For other services like taxis or guided tours, a small tip is also appreciated.

8. Staying Safe with Your Money
Always be mindful of your belongings and money, especially in crowded areas. Use hotel safes to store your valuables and only carry what you need for the day. Be cautious at ATMs, and try to use machines located in well-lit, busy areas.

9. Useful Contacts and Resources
For currency conversion rates, apps like XE Currency can be very helpful. For any banking issues, having the contact number of your bank's international customer service can save you time and stress.

By keeping these tips in mind, you can manage your money effectively and enjoy your time in Dordogne without financial worries. Embrace the charming experiences of this beautiful region with confidence, knowing your finances are well in hand.

Safety and Health Considerations

The Dordogne Valley, with its picturesque landscapes and charming villages, is a delightful destination for travelers. However, like any travel destination, it's essential to consider safety and health factors to ensure a smooth and enjoyable trip.

Safety Tips:

1. Stay Informed: Before traveling to Dordogne, research the current safety situation and any travel advisories issued by your government. Stay updated on local news and developments during your stay.

2. Secure Your Belongings: While Dordogne is relatively safe, petty theft can occur, especially in tourist areas. Keep your belongings secure and be mindful of your surroundings, particularly in crowded places and public transportation.

3. Be Street Smart: Avoid walking alone in unfamiliar or poorly lit areas, especially at night. Stick to well-lit and populated streets, and trust your instincts if a situation feels unsafe.

4. Follow Local Laws and Customs: Respect local laws, customs, and traditions to avoid any unnecessary complications. Familiarize yourself with basic French phrases to communicate effectively with locals if needed.

Health Considerations:

1. Stay Hydrated: The Dordogne region can experience warm temperatures, especially during the summer months. Drink plenty of water to stay hydrated, especially if you're engaging in outdoor activities or sightseeing.

2. Sun Protection: Protect yourself from the sun's harmful rays by wearing sunscreen, a hat, and sunglasses, especially during peak sun hours. Seek shade when necessary, and stay hydrated to prevent heat-related illnesses.

3. Food and Water Safety: Enjoy the delicious local cuisine, but be cautious of food hygiene practices, particularly at street stalls and local markets. Drink bottled water or opt for beverages served in sealed containers to avoid waterborne illnesses.

4. Medical Care: Familiarize yourself with the location of medical facilities, pharmacies, and emergency services in the area you're visiting. Carry any necessary medications with you and consider purchasing travel insurance for peace of mind.

By following these safety and health considerations, you can enjoy your time in the Dordogne Valley to the fullest while ensuring your well-being throughout your journey.

Emergency Contacts

While traveling in the Dordogne Valley, it's essential to have access to emergency contacts in case you encounter any unforeseen situations. Here are some key contacts you should keep handy during your trip:

1. Emergency Services (Police, Fire, Ambulance): In case of emergencies requiring immediate assistance, dial 112, the universal emergency number in Europe. This will connect you to the appropriate emergency services, including police, fire, and ambulance.

2. Local Police Station: Familiarize yourself with the contact information for the nearest police station in the area you're staying. They can assist with reporting incidents, filing complaints, or seeking help in non-emergency situations.

3. Medical Emergency Services: If you require urgent medical assistance, dial 15 to reach SAMU (Service d'Aide Médicale Urgente), the French emergency medical service. They can dispatch ambulances and provide medical advice over the phone.

4. Fire Department (Pompiers): Dial 18 for fire emergencies

5. Hospital or Medical Clinic: Identify the nearest hospital or medical clinic to your accommodation. In case of non-life-threatening medical issues or injuries, you can visit these facilities for treatment.

6. Embassy or Consulate: If you're a foreign national traveling in the Dordogne Valley, know the contact information for your country's embassy or consulate in France. They can assist you with passport issues, legal matters, and other consular services.

7. Travel Insurance Provider: Keep the contact details for your travel insurance provider easily accessible. In case of emergencies requiring medical assistance or travel assistance, contact them for guidance and support.

8. Local Tourist Information Office: The local tourist information office can provide valuable assistance and information for travelers. They can offer guidance on nearby attractions, transportation options, and local services.

By having these emergency contacts readily available, you can ensure prompt assistance and support during any unexpected situations while exploring the beautiful Dordogne Valley. Remember to program these numbers into your phone and keep a written list in case of emergencies.

Useful Websites and Apps

When traveling to the Dordogne Valley, having access to useful websites and apps can enhance your experience and make your trip more enjoyable. Here are some recommendations to help you navigate your journey:

1. Google Maps: This versatile mapping app is indispensable for exploring the Dordogne region. Whether you're walking, driving, or using public transportation, Google Maps provides

accurate directions, real-time traffic updates, and detailed information about nearby attractions, restaurants, and services.

2. TripAdvisor: Use TripAdvisor to discover top-rated restaurants, and accommodations in the Dordogne Valley. Browse traveler reviews, ratings, and to make informed decisions about where to visit and dine during your stay.

3. Airbnb: If you prefer unique and personalized accommodations, consider using Airbnb to find local hosts offering vacation rentals, apartments, and unique stays in the Dordogne area. This platform allows you to connect directly with hosts and book accommodations tailored to your preferences.

4. Dordogne Tourism :Visit the official tourism website of the Dordogne Valley to access comprehensive information about the region's attractions, events, accommodations, and activities. The website often features travel guides, maps, and special offers to help you plan your trip.
Website:www.guide-du-perigord.com/en/:
5. Weather.com: Check the weather forecast for the Dordogne Valley on Weather.com before embarking on outdoor activities or excursions. Knowing the weather conditions in advance can help you pack appropriately and plan your itinerary accordingly.

6. Trainline: If you're planning to travel by train within France or to neighboring countries, use Trainline to book train tickets, check schedules, and track train statuses. This convenient app

streamlines the process of arranging train travel and ensures a smooth journey.

7. Duolingo: Brush up on your French language skills with Duolingo, a popular language-learning app. Whether you're a beginner or looking to improve your proficiency, Duolingo offers fun and interactive lessons that can help you communicate more effectively during your trip.

8. Airbnb Experiences: Explore unique activities and experiences offered by local hosts through Airbnb Experiences. From cooking classes to guided tours, Airbnb Experiences allow you to immerse yourself in the culture and lifestyle of the Dordogne Valley with the guidance of knowledgeable hosts.

9. IGN Maps:
Website:(www.ign.fr)
   - The National Institute of Geographic and Forest Information (IGN) offers detailed topographic maps that are perfect for hiking and exploring the natural landscapes of Dordogne.
By utilizing these websites and apps, you can enhance your travel experience in the Dordogne Valley and make the most of your time exploring this charming region. Whether you're seeking recommendations, navigating transportation, or immersing yourself in local culture, these resources can be invaluable tools for a memorable trip.

CONCLUSION

As your journey through the Dordogne Valley comes to a close, it's time to reflect on the myriad experiences, sights, and flavors that have woven together to create unforgettable memories. From the rolling vineyards and medieval castles to the charming villages and culinary delights, the Dordogne has captivated your senses and left an indelible mark on your heart.

As you bid farewell to this enchanting region, remember that the Dordogne is not just a place on a map – it's a tapestry of stories waiting to be discovered, A hidden gem mine that's just waiting to be discovered. Whether you've indulged in Michelin-starred feasts, meandered through bustling markets, or embarked on outdoor adventures, your journey has been a testament to the richness and diversity of this corner of France.

But perhaps the true magic of the Dordogne lies not just in its breathtaking landscapes or delectable cuisine, but in the connections forged with fellow travelers and locals alike. From chance encounters in charming cafes to shared moments of wonder in ancient caves, the Dordogne has brought people together from all walks of life, united by a shared love for adventure and discovery.

As you return home with a suitcase full of souvenirs and a heart full of memories, carry with you the spirit of the Dordogne – a spirit of curiosity, of appreciation for the simple joys of life, and of openness to new experiences. Whether you find yourself reminiscing about lazy afternoons by the river, savoring the taste of freshly baked croissants, or marveling at centuries-old architecture, know that the Dordogne will always have a unique place in your bag of travel tricks.

So, until we meet again, dear traveler, may the spirit of the Dordogne continue to inspire and enrich your adventures, wherever they may lead. Bon voyage, and may your next journey be filled with as much joy, discovery, and magic as your time in the Dordogne Valley.

11024151R00075